i shot andy warhol

I SHOT ANDY WARHOL

Mary Harron

and

Daniel Minahan

Grove Press

New York

Published simultaneously in Canada
Printed in the United States of America

FIRST EDITION

Library of Congress Cataloging-in-Publication Data

Harron, Mary.
  I shot Andy Warhol / written by Mary Harron and Daniel Minahan.—
1st ed.
     p.   cm.
  Shooting script for the film.
  Includes: SCUM manifesto / Valerie Solanas.
  ISBN 0–8021–3491–2
  1. Solanas, Valerie—Drama. 2. Warhol, Andy, 1928– —Drama.
3. Sex role. I. Minahan, Daniel. II. Solanas, Valerie. SCUM
manifesto. III. I shot Andy Warhol (Motion picture) IV. Title.
PN1997.I19 1996
791.43'72—dc20   96–18202

Design by Laura Hammond Hough

Grove Press
841 Broadway
New York, NY 10003

10 9 8 7 6 5 4 3 2 1

Contents

Introduction:
On Valerie Solanas

There is one question that I am always asked about *I Shot Andy Warhol*, and that is how I became interested in Valerie Solanas. I actually do have an answer because it was a very specific and vivid moment, although now somewhat blurred by the retelling.

What I can't remember is the date, whether it was in 1987 or 1988. I know that Andy Warhol had recently died, because I had just finished researching a television documentary about him. I was walking to work through South London one morning, and as usual, I glanced in the window of the Brixton Bookshop. There, before me, was a copy of the *SCUM Manifesto*. I couldn't believe my eyes.

I knew all about the *SCUM Manifesto*, or thought I did. Valerie Solanas, this crazy woman who shot Warhol, was the leader and sole member of a revolutionary organization called the Society for Cutting up Men (SCUM). She used to sell the yet unpublished "SCUM Manifesto" on street corners to indifferent passersby: it was, it had to be, a deranged rant, whose blurry mimeographed pages had been lost in the gutters of the 1960s. And yet clearly it had survived, because a women's collective had just reprinted it. I bought a copy and read it on the subway, an experience that literally changed my life. Nothing I read had ever affected me so profoundly.

> Life in this society being, at best, an utter bore and no aspect of society being at all relevant to women, there remains to civic-minded, responsible, thrill-seeking females only to overthrow the government, eliminate

the money system, institute complete automation and destroy the male sex.

First, there was the tone of voice: The *SCUM Manifesto* is a paean of hatred, a fifty-page diatribe blaming men for everything that is wrong with the modern world, yet the tone is deadpan, icily logical, elegantly comic; a strange juxtaposition, as if Oscar Wilde had decided to become a terrorist. I was stunned because in all the accounts I had read of the shooting—and as a researcher I had read many—no one had said that Valerie Solanas was talented or funny.

I was both attracted and scared by her writing. In *The Prisoner of Sex,* Norman Mailer calls Valerie the Robespierre of feminism, and if taken literally, her *Manifesto* does advocate male genocide.

The *Manifesto* envisions a war between men and women—a real war, as opposed to the symbolic struggles that have characterized the last few decades. It ends with the suggestion that in order to create a healthy society, men should be exterminated but not all men: some will be saved, including good scientists, supportive journalists and publishers, "faggots," and philanthropists. These lucky few will be saved as long as they help to propagate the message that "a woman's primary goal in life should be to squash the male sex." Such passages have the abstract quality of a revenge fantasy: Valerie seems never to have considered the implications of what it would be like literally to kill men. She even presents violence as a male aberration: "A woman not only takes her identity and individuality for granted, but knows instinctively the only wrong's to hurt others and the meaning of life is love."

I don't know, and will probably never know, under what circumstances Valerie Solanas wrote the *SCUM Manifesto,* but it reads as if it was written in one ecstatic, vindictive rush. Critic B. Ruby Rich calls her feminism's Joan of Arc. Valerie, who grew up in a world where male supremacy was taken for granted, was possessed by a vision that everything she had been told about the natural order of society was a lie. This situation, where one person's view of the world is utterly at variance with the society around them, is one definition of madness, but it is also what was once called prophecy.

The *Manifesto* has a primal kick; it reached a core of anger I didn't know I possessed. On first reading it, I thought, "I have never had the courage even to think some of these things, and Valerie Solanas only had that courage because she had cut her moorings and separated herself from traditional feminine virtues such as fairness, compassion, empathy." That separation allowed her to see, coldly and cruelly, just how the power structures lay. The *Manifesto* continuously mocks "niceness, politeness and dignity" as the hallmarks of the toady, and it asserts that male supremacy survived by flattering women with their own virtues, with their humility, altruism, self-denial, all of which cast the victim's role in the most flattering light.

The power of the *Manifesto* isn't just the attack on men but also the attack on the way women behave with men; it investigates the psychic damage done to both sexes. Some of Valerie's harshest judgments are reserved for women, for the collaborator with male supremacy she calls "[p]assive, rattle-headed Daddy's Girl, ever eager for approval, for a pat on the head, for the respect of any passing piece of garbage . . . soother of the weary, apey brow, booster of the puny ego, appreciator of the contemptible, a hot water bottle with tits."

If Valerie Solanas, an obscure lunatic who went down in history simply as the Factory reject who failed to kill Warhol—a walk-on with a gun—was capable of writing like this, I wondered, what does it mean about all the bag ladies we pass every day in the street? (Even now, when I walk by a woman muttering to herself, I think, "Valerie.") Are the streets and shelters filled with neglected genius? It made me wonder about blighted talents, vanished possibilities, and what might be lurking in the great host of humanity we call failures.

My first thought was to make a classic British arts documentary about Valerie Solanas, with all the usual high seriousness and reverent attention to detail but focused on someone that society had deemed worthless. Not surprisingly, this proved hard to sell. After four years the one producer at the BBC who had encouraged the project, Anthony Wall, was able to scrape together some development money, and in New York, a brilliant researcher, Diane Tucker, took on the task of uncovering Valerie's story when there was very little published information, no cooperation from the family, and when Valerie seemed to have vanished without trace.

If Valerie Solanas had been born just a few years later, her incendiary writing might have found its audience. Even as a celebrity assassin, she was in the wrong time. Now a Valerie Solanas would have a book contract; her case would be debated on talk radio and daytime television talk shows; and she would be interviewed by *People* magazine. Then, however, there was nothing. Warhol may have envisioned and defined the cult of celebrity, but in 1968, it had yet to take hold. The result is that there is very little record of Valerie Solanas; even at the Factory, a place where everyone was obsessively photographed and recorded, there are no photos and just one available piece of film: her appearance in *I, a Man,* a witty scene-stealing performance where she demolishes the male protagonist, Tom Baker.

Diane started the search by interviewing most of the prominent feminists of the sixties. The first surprise was that very few had actually met Valerie Solanas. Some were dismissive; others said the *Manifesto* was a milestone because its fury and outrageousness had shifted the boundaries of accepted behavior, had made normal female anger seem reasonable in comparison. But all agreed that Valerie had never aligned herself with any feminist group: she always walked through life alone.

There were no political comrades and no close friends, or none that Diane and I knew of. That left the archives. We moved on to the main reference rooms of the New York Public Library, along with the other obsessives: the conspiracy theorists, the old men with shopping bags stuffed full of newspaper clippings, the nervous girls researching the Celestine Prophecies. Diane sometimes found herself sitting next to a woman who held metal kitchen utensils over her head to ward off harmful vibrations as she was reading.

Diane spent days in the twilight of the microfilm machines, getting seasick from the newsprint blurring in and out of focus. The best account came from a story in the *New York Post* by Judy Michaelson, who uncovered Valerie's early life. Valerie Jean Solanas was born on April 9, 1936, in Atlantic City, the eldest of the two daughters of Dorothy Biondi and Louis Solanas, a bartender, now divorced: "There is the sense, in talking to family and those close to the family, of a 'bad seed,' the child who was always difficult. . . . When she was 15, she got 'involved with a sailor,' said someone who knows the family well. 'Since then she's been pretty much against men. Oh, just say the whole deal was taken care of by the parents.'"

Through the BBC, we placed want ads in newspapers in New York, San Francisco, and New Jersey, but they turned up only one person who had actually known Valerie. Clara Shields lived next door to Valerie when they were both children. A kindly middle-aged woman in an immaculate small house filled with ornaments and family photos, she remembered Valerie with a mixture of affection and bemusement. I found this to be true of those who had known her when she was young, whereas those who had only known her later on, just before or after the shooting, tended to regard her as mad and scary.

The street where they lived is now a bleak row of slum houses right by the boardwalk, almost in the shadow of the Trump Taj Mahal casino. Back then, it was respectable postwar blue-collar housing, with a mix of races and nationalities. Valerie was then living with her maternal grandparents, the Biondis, because her mother was living in Washington, D.C.; Valerie told Clara proudly that her mother was working as a nurse. All the children used to play by the boardwalk, and Clara remembered that one day a boy was tormenting a younger girl. Valerie rounded on him and beat the shit out of him. Clara also recalled that Valerie had been thrown out of Holy Cross Academy for hitting a nun. She was a volatile girl.

Tracing Valerie's life was also an attempt to trace at what point it went wrong. Of all the variables—bad home life, poverty, psychological instability, born in the wrong time—probably the most damaging were the things that happened to her at the start. On June 26, 1968, two psychiatrists who interviewed Valerie when she was at Elmhurst Hospital Psychiatric Ward wrote a report describing "a rather pitiful childhood, including parental conflict, sexual molestation by her father, and frequent separation from her home." Valerie described a wild adolescence involving shoplifting and other petty crimes and, by the age of thirteen, "many sexual experiences." At fourteen, she was sent to a boarding school, which provided a temporary salvation. Her grades improved, and she had her first lesbian experiences: many years later she told her publisher Maurice Girodias that she had only been in love once in her life, with a girl she met at boarding school.

On returning to her family in Washington, she attended Oxon Hill High School in Maryland, where a classmate later recalled that Valerie was often the butt of fellow students' jokes. One day a student put a tack on her chair. She swung round and slugged the boy behind her, who turned out to be the wrong one. There was more trouble in the family, and Valerie left home to live on her own while she was still in high school. Her principal's report explained that "she lacks financial support at home, and is determined to get an education." In 1954, Valerie entered the University of Maryland, which had the obvious attraction of being virtually free—her fees were only fifty dollars a term—where she majored in psychology.

When Valerie was interrogated after the shooting, she told both the police and the psychiatrists who examined her that she was born on April 9, 1940, which would make her twenty-eight years old. In fact, she was thirty-two. The four years' difference is important: Valerie was a product, not of the sixties, but of the fifties. Born in 1936, she entered college in 1954. If she had been born four years later, her time at the university would have coincided with the Kennedy era. She might have found a more sympathetic atmosphere at college, might have stayed in academia and—who knows?—might have survived to become a more apocalyptic Camille Paglia. Instead, Valerie's college years belonged to Eisenhower.

What this meant can be judged by examining a photograph of the University of Maryland's class of '58. This was in the days before youth culture had really taken hold, and the girls have the curiously middle-aged look of fifties' students, uniformly dressed in Peter Pan collars, twinsets, and pearls. There in the middle of these bright and wholesome smiles and freshly permed hair is Valerie Solanas, in a work shirt and dungarees, glowering at the camera. She was an open lesbian at a time when most students were still agonizing over sex before marriage.

Valerie majored in psychology and made the honor society Psi Chi. Her scientific training would feed into her theories: the *SCUM Manifesto* is based on a theory of male genetic inferiority. In the *Manifesto*, she states that "[t]he male is a biological accident: the y (male) gene is an incomplete x (female) gene, that is, has an incomplete set of chromosomes." Valerie's almost naive fifties' faith in the power of science and technology underpins her *Manifesto*'s utopianism: We will find ways of mechanizing society so that no one need work, and the money system can be abolished. Babies can be made in test tubes.

In exchange for research credits, Valerie worked as an assistant to Dr. Robert Brush in the experimental animal laboratory, helping in his work "on the differences between animals that learn and do not learn to avoid electric shock." Brush recently described Valerie as "a very interesting, unusual student. I would use the words *diffident* and *brash* at the same time." He found her bright and dedicated, if difficult. "She was as rebellious as hell . . . she had a chip on her shoulder a mile high. [But] she liked me, and I liked her. I had a warm spot for her—I felt she'd come up the hard way."

As we talked, Dr. Brush told me that he had a sudden flashback to the last time someone called to ask him about Valerie Solanas. It was in 1968, the day after the shooting: "I said, 'Oh, my God, poor Valerie.' The reporter told me I was the first person she'd talked to who had any sympathy for her."

The University of Maryland was probably the first place Valerie had found anything like a group of sympathetic souls. Although it was a fairly conservative campus, there was a group of more questioning, intellectual students, mainly psychology majors, interested in art, poetry, modern jazz—the staples of the urban coffeehouse scene.

Jean Holroyd, a psychology major who was friendly with Valerie, said of the group: "We were bright, not rebellious. *She* was rebellious . . . she was very intelligent, very bright, [had] a good sense of humor." And she was filled with anger: Valerie was continually hauled in for student counseling and once threw a table over during a session. Jean recalled that Valerie seemed older, more hardened and cynical than the other students. "She'd been on her own a long time . . . [it seemed she'd had] a very, very hard life and didn't develop the necessary trust."

Another friend, who was a disc jockey in Washington when I spoke to him, remembered that she was one of only two students in their class who had a 4.4 grade point average. Valerie had admitted to him that she was working her way through school by prostitution; she had no support from home, and money was always a problem. One summer she suggested to him that he come up to Atlantic City with her and find work as a waiter while she worked as a cocktail waitress and turned tricks: whenever possible, she would get her tricks drunk and roll them.

She told him she had left home early; "she mentioned unwanted sex with her family—a father or stepfather—when she was quite young." This friend was intimidated by Valerie, who was a little older, and one night when she suggested they sleep together, he was somewhat alarmed. He was at her place where she was cooking on a little hot plate, and she suddenly asked, "How would you like to spend the night with me?" He said, somewhat nervously, "Valerie, I thought you liked girls." "Everyone likes a change once in a while," she answered. It was, he said, a clinical experience.

She lived extremely frugally and expected her friends to look after her if they went out. At one time she was sharing a small basement apartment with three other girls. When one of them offended her, Valerie gleefully reported, she peed in the girl's orange juice and put it back in the fridge. Clearly, Valerie's vindictive streak was already well developed, but she also showed an intense neediness. "If you helped her once, she was going to be back for more of the same . . . I tried to cut back without cutting back [completely]. Val sensed a mild rebuff and she went back completely and she wouldn't ask for anything—which wasn't what I had intended at all."

In 1958, she went to the University of Minnesota to do her graduate work. According to the 1968 psychiatric report, she got bored and left, after which "she travelled through various parts of the country and lived with several men, none of whom she liked." Whatever else happened in those missing years, by 1965, she was living a full-fledged bohemian existence in Greenwich Village. Her days were spent drifting, panhandling on street corners, passing the afternoon over a cup of coffee in a cheap restaurant. She liked to hang out, to "shoot the shit": I have a mental picture of her lying on a bed in a cheap hotel room, surrounded by old newspapers and piles of manuscript. When she couldn't collect enough money panhandling, she would turn tricks.

Eventually, Valerie moved into the Hotel Earle just off Washington Square Park. The Earle was a kind of terminus for deviants, with separate wings for lesbians and drag queens. There she met Candy Cane, later known as Candy Darling, the beautiful drag queen who became a Warhol Superstar. Candy and Valerie had a mutual friend, a bisexual prostitute called English Pat, and they all frequented the Eighth Street Nedick's, which was painted a livid orange.

We had two sources for those years. One was Candy's best friend, Jeremiah Newton, who now runs a film program at New York University. Jeremiah provided several scenes in the film (including his memoir of Valerie's disastrous appearance on the *Alan Burke Show*), as well as Candy's diaries and letters. The other was an article Valerie wrote about her life on the streets called "A Young Girl's Primer, or How to Attain to the Leisure Class." It was published in 1966 in *Cavalier* magazine, a men's magazine with aspirations to hipness. (Not long before the shooting, she tried to interest the magazine in a regular column to be called "Lesbian at Large," but sadly, it declined.) The "Primer" is a wonderful piece of comic writing, brutal yet elegant, like a lesbian Joe Orton. After college, its narrator explains, she sets out to search for:

> a way of life appropriate to a young woman of taste, cultivation and sensitivity. . . . I finally hit upon an excellent paying occupation, challenging to the ingenuity, dealing on one's own terms with people and affording independence, flexible hours, great stability and, most important, a large amount of leisure time, an occupation highly appropriate to female sensibilities. I contemplate my good fortune as I begin work for the day:
>> "Pardon me, Sir, do you have fifteen cents?"
>> "Sure, Sweetie, here." It's my wild body—gets them almost every time.

The narrator continues panhandling, stopping only to refuse money to a friend, until she meets a man who wants to watch a lesbian show, "Room for three at the Hotel Earle," which pays enough for her to take three days off to write. When the money runs out, she's back on the streets: "I pass a sidewalk speaker. I'll grab a listen. A socialist. I listen awhile, then leave, continuing to do my bit toward bringing about socialism by remaining off the labor market. But first a few little acquisitions from the 5 & 10, since it's right here. I enter, considering what more I, as a woman, can do for my country—shoplift."

Scorning a woman handing out advertisements to a lecture to men only, the narrator then tries to teach another girl the ways of panhandling but decides "[t]he girl's an incompetent and she'll wind up with a job." The narrator describes another maneuver Valerie allegedly used in real life: selling conversation for money, an hour's worth for six bucks, any topic, but sex is a favorite, "and for an additional four bucks I do illustrations on a napkin." She sneers at another girl handing out leaflets: "Nice middle-class lady," one of Betty Friedan's "privileged, educated girls." Like the speaker in the *Manifesto,* the narrator despises ladylike women who become involved in politics.

The persona Valerie adopts here—confident, cool, swinging, in charge—is an idealized self, the version of herself she most wanted to be. In the "Primer," her character seems to float through the streets, free of obligations, emotional ties, vulnerability, and pain. "A Young Girl's Primer" may give a lighthearted view of Valerie's life on the streets, but the reality included sordid rooms, inadequate food, and performing blow jobs to pay the rent. The *Manifesto,* which was probably written a year or so later, reveals her contempt for that life and a frustration that is about to explode: "SCUM doesn't yet prevail; SCUM's still in the gutter of our society, which, if it's not deflected from its present course and if the Bomb doesn't drop on it, will hump itself to death."

There were times when Valerie slept on rooftops and ate what was left on other peoples' plates at the Automat. Perhaps even worse for Valerie was the obscurity, the lack of any sense of importance or respect or influence. It wasn't an easy life for an ambitious young woman who must have been looking for a way, any way, to crawl out of the shadows into the light. Then she met Andy Warhol.

The photographer Nat Finkelstein said he was the one who first brought Valerie to the Factory, and that it was something of an act of revenge, since he knew how difficult Valerie was. Why did she want to meet Warhol in the first place? It could not have been because of his work: she was a political creature, a sociologist, not much interested in art. It must have been because she found there an opportunity, or the possibility of one, that she could see nowhere else. She seems to have been attracted by his power and influence, the reflective glow of his celebrity, his ability to get things done. And where else could Valerie have gone? Certainly not the New Left; in 1967, it was as sexist as the Pentagon.

Gerard Malanga, Warhol's chief assistant during the Factory glory days, remembered her as "a fringe person" at the Factory. Shy and isolated, she rarely talked to other members of the entourage. "She'd have one on ones with Andy—she was always trying to solicit Andy." She was desperate for him to produce her play, "Up Your Ass." She left the script with Warhol, and then it disappeared, like so much else, into the general Factory clutter. This would have disastrous consequences later, as Valerie, in the grip of an increasing paranoia, became convinced that Warhol had stolen the play. Malanga points out that it was unlikely they would ever have used "Up Your Ass," because in that period, they didn't use real scripts—most of their dialogue was improvised.

The lost manuscript of Valerie's play became our Holy Grail. I had given up hope of finding it, when back in London, I had an urgent message to phone Diane Tucker in New York. After calling every collector of pornography and erotica in the country, she found one who had a copy of "Up Your Ass." It turned out to be the story of a prostitute, Bongi Perez (a character much like the persona Valerie displays in "A Young Girl's Primer"), and her encounters with different people she meets in the street. The play is more awkward than her prose but is filled with snappy dialogue and outrageous ideas; it could certainly have held its own in the off-Broadway theater of the time.

Later, we found out that another copy of "Up Your Ass" had surfaced. Some time after Warhol's death, a trunk was sent to Billy Name, who had designed the silver Factory and who had acted as its house photographer and general custodian in the mid-sixties. There at the bottom was the copy of the play that Valerie gave Andy, and whose loss had such terrible consequences. Billy had loved the play, and he remembered Valerie as a talented woman who didn't know how to push herself. The Factory was a chorus of narcissists, all crying for attention, and those who cried loudest got their projects made.

The film director Paul Morrissey, whose star was rising at the Factory at this time, despised Valerie. He thought of her as a pathetic street person, almost mentally defective, and was astonished when I said she had worked on a master's degree in psychology. He has always defended Warhol against accusations of mistreating the people around him: "Andy was like a social worker . . . Andy was nice to everyone." When I asked why Warhol had taken the time to talk to Valerie if she was so awful, Morrissey gave the most revealing insight I had yet encountered into the Valerie-Warhol relationship: that Warhol had seen something of himself in Valerie. "He was very limited [in social situations]; he was so difficult—she was so offbeat."

When Andy Warhol looked into the eyes of Valerie Solanas, he would have seen much more of himself than when he looked in the eyes of a beautiful debutante like Edie Sedgewick or of one of the gorgeous male hustlers who decorated the Factory. Warhol and Valerie had much in common: both were Catholic, born into blue-collar families; had spent their childhood in poverty; were intellectually precocious; and had experienced being tormented at school. Perhaps most important, both claimed to have rejected sex, although for different reasons: Valerie had had too much sex; Warhol, too little.

Valerie's rejection of sex was not so much based on a visceral hatred of the act itself as on a hatred of what sex means in the power struggle between men and women. Sex is a physical and emotional need, which for Valerie meant weakness, dependency, and defeat. For Valerie, sexual romance was the Trojan horse through which women allowed themselves to be conquered. Stephen Koch writes in his 1973 study of Warhol's films, *Stargazer:* "Valerie lives in terror of dependence: That is what the *S.C.U.M. Manifesto* is about, an absolute terror before the experience of need. Like Warhol, Solanis [*sic*] is obsessed with an image of autonomy, except that . . . she has played the obsession desperately, rather than with Warhol's famous cool."

In 1967, Valerie Solanas met a man who would affect her destiny just as much as Warhol. This was Maurice Girodias, the brilliant and notorious French publisher who had started the Olympia Press. A hopeless businessman, he had fled multiple bankruptcies in Paris to start up an American operation. Valerie was struck by the advertisement in the back pages of U.S. Olympia paperbacks:

NOTICE TO UNKNOWN WRITERS
The Olympia Press, founded in Paris (on a shoestring) by Maurice Girodias in 1953, allegedly to pervert American tourists into a pornographic way of life, published *The Story of O* in 1954, *Lolita* and *The Ginger Man* in 1955, all of de Sade's novels and most of Henry Miller's best works, *Candy* in 1958, *Naked Lunch* and Durrell's *Black Book* in 1959—not to speak of dozens of other interesting authors, masterpieces and diversions. . . . We are not interested in anyone famous, or half famous. Our function is to discover talent. Unknown writers are our specialty. You have been rejected by all existing publishers: well and good, you have a chance with us. We read everything—promptly, discriminatively and optimistically.

Valerie seemed to have found the perfect publisher. She discovered his existence when they both lived at the Chelsea Hotel. She left him a note explaining she was a writer, and asking to see him. In his introduction to the first edition of the *SCUM Mani-*

festo, Girodias recalls that "[w]e met. Her manner was friendly, lively, and she had a sense of humor—which somewhat took the edge off the anti-masculine doctrine she proceeded to preach to me. The title of her play, *Up Your Ass,* was sufficiently indicative of her iconoclastic disposition, and naturally I sympathized as I was supposed to. The play was rather clever, and I found it amusingly wild. I also found myself, quite to my surprise, in agreement with what I understood of her theories."

Intellectually, Valerie and Girodias had far more in common than Valerie and Warhol. Both loved words, and took pride in being subversive, what Girodias called "the urge to attack the Universal Establishment with all the means at my disposal." The fact that he was a pornographer would not have bothered her at all.

Girodias believed that a society that frustrated women's talents was sterile and oppressive for both sexes, and having a good sense of the zeitgeist, he could feel the tremors of the women's movement. In Paris, Girodias had encouraged women to write erotica; he loved women and prided himself on understanding and appreciating them, although that appreciation was of the old school, inextricably bound up with sex and romance. Of anyone Valerie met in that time in New York, he came the closest to appreciating her talents, albeit without ever truly understanding her.

Many years later, in a radio interview in Paris, he remembered her as "extremely energetic and brutal, like New York girls who beg and live by their wits are . . . she was naive, she was very smart, she could not come to terms with these contradictory forces: the fact that she did not look quite like a woman but neither like a man . . . I would not have married her, of course, but I did really like her; I found her very funny."

He asked Valerie to write a novel about her experiences, and to celebrate, he took her for dinner at the restaurant next door to the Chelsea Hotel, El Quixote. She astonished him by turning up in makeup and "a magnificent red dress." The contract was signed in August 1967. Girodias paid her a $500 advance against royalties, with the promise of a further $1,500 in installments.

Shortly after signing the contract, she appeared in Warhol's movie *I, a Man*. A few weeks later, Valerie invited Girodias to accompany her to a private screening at the Factory of her scene in *I, a Man*. Warhol was there, and Girodias noted that she seemed relaxed and friendly in his company. But like many of Warhol's performers, before and after, she came to feel that he had exploited her by paying so little: she asked him for money, always a dangerous move at the Factory. "Talking to him is like talking to a chair . . . a snake couldn't live on what he pays out," she complained. She became a pest with her continuous phone calls, and one day, to Warhol's terror, she phoned him at home. He had no idea how she had got the number.

As Warhol retreated from Valerie, the elaborate defense mechanism that he had instituted at the Factory came into play, and she was frozen out. There were other difficult and unstable people at the Factory; why did they survive when Valerie didn't? They were "fabulous," whereas she wasn't beautiful or rich or amusing in the accepted Factory sense. She was too serious, not to say, monomaniacal. She believed in politics. She was a revolutionary, whereas Warhol had no desire to change the status quo. The Factory had a reputation as the most outrageous place in America, but it couldn't handle Valerie Solanas.

In Warhol, Valerie had found a father figure who eerily resembled the archetypal daddy she excoriated in the *SCUM Manifesto*: "For the kid to want Daddy's approval it must respect Daddy, and being garbage, Daddy can make sure that he is respected only by remaining aloof, by distantness, by acting on the precept 'familiarity breeds contempt,' which is, of course, true if one is contemptible."

Valerie did not write a novel, and her relationship with her publisher deteriorated. A connection had been made in Valerie's mind between her two mentors, Warhol and Girodias, who she came to believe were united in conspiracy against her. Warhol had stolen her play; Girodias had tried to tie her up with his "greasy contract." Girodias would steal the *SCUM Manifesto*, so Warhol could make a film of it.

By the fall of 1967, Valerie had been kicked out of the Chelsea Hotel. Since she still had not produced a line of the contracted novel, she asked Girodias if he would publish the *Manifesto* instead. After some wrangling and aggressive letters on her part, he agreed, but she then balked at the new contract he had prepared. At their meeting about the new contract, she launched into a furious diatribe against Warhol, calling him a vulture and a thief. Girodias wrote later, "This did not seem to make any sense since she really had nothing anyone would want to steal."

She began writing hate letters to Girodias at his office, addressing him as "lowly toad," and mixing threats and insults with desperate pleas for attention. One night she called him at 4 A.M., "remarking that I had a big enough place at the Chelsea and asking me rather sweetly if she could move in." A few days later, he received this letter:

> M. G.—
> I don't intend to write the novel. You can publish
> "SCUM Manifesto" in it's [*sic*] place. The "SCUM
> Manifesto" is now yours, to have & to hold—
> forever.
>
> Valerie Solanas

It seems characteristic of Valerie that she would fight so desperately over a contract and then give up all at once, as if on a whim: a pendulum swing between hostility and passivity, between SCUM revolutionary and Daddy's girl.

The most haunting portrait of Valerie in the final months leading up to the shooting comes from an article in the *Village Voice* titled "Scum Goddess, a Winter Memory of Valerie Solanis [*sic*]." The interview was done the winter before the shooting but published only after it. The freelance writer Robert Marmarstein had observed Valerie panhandling, bought and read the *Manifesto,* and arranged to interview her. They met at the corner of Twenty-third Street and Eighth Avenue, near the Chelsea Hotel.

She wore a sailor's pea jacket and her trademark cap, and shivered against the cold. They ended up in a small Chinese restaurant where Valerie wolfed down a steak, badgering the waiter for more bread and french fries. She seems to have been always hungry.

Valerie and Marmarstein argued about SCUM, and she disagreed with him about the value of peaceful revolution: "Marching, demonstrating. That's for little old ladies who aren't serious. SCUM is a criminal organization, not a civil disobedience luncheon club." Suddenly, she turned to him, and asked where he lived and if he would like a roommate. "How about it? I'll keep out of your way. I wouldn't make a bad-looking roommate either, would I?" She also told him that Warhol was going to produce "Up Your Ass" in an off-off-Broadway theater, although by this time she and Warhol were no longer speaking.

A month later Marmarstein saw Valerie on a street corner on another freezing cold night. She sat in his car for a few minutes to get warm. He watched her go back on the street, with her pile of unsold *Manifesto*s, as indifferent passersby walked past and she earnestly tried to explain her ideas to a young couple.

Valerie disappeared for a few months to California, where her younger sister was living. We have been unable to trace any record of Valerie during that time. In her only interview on the subject, Valerie's mother mentioned a friend who took care of Valerie and gave her money. This may have been a young man named Jeffrey LeGear, who spent time with Valerie in Los Angeles, and who posted $10,000 bail for her after the shooting.

Apart from a few vitriolic phone calls, Girodias heard nothing from Valerie until he read about the shooting while he was on a plane back from Montreal. At that time, he experienced what others must have felt as they thought back on the *Manifesto*: "But no, it *was* a joke; it had to be! She could not possibly have convinced herself that she was able to carry out the greatest genocide in the history of mankind [single-handedly]!"

That spring, Warhol had moved the Factory from the old silver-foiled palace of excess to a new upscale location. The combined influences of Paul Morrissey and Fred Hughes had culminated in a search for order and a more businesslike approach to art and film. Warhol and his entourage were already anticipating the seventies: the new Factory was all retro chic, with white walls, polished wooden floors, art deco desks, and a new door policy with a bias in favor of the rich and famous. On June 3, 1968, Valerie Solanas waited outside these new offices at 33 Union Square.

She had made one visit there already but been turned away by Morrissey, who had no patience with her: "No panhandling today, Valerie." Warhol arrived, and she rode up in the elevator with him and his assistant Jed Johnson. It was noticed that she was very heavily dressed for the warm summer weather, and that she was wearing lipstick and makeup. The last recorded time she had put on makeup was for her dinner with Girodias: it was evidently something she saved for important social occasions.

In the Factory, after some desultory conversation, she shot Warhol three times. Only one bullet hit, but its wild trajectory caused enormous damage, entering through the left lung and hitting the spleen, stomach, liver, and esophagus before penetrating the right lung and exiting from the side. She then turned the gun on a visiting art dealer, Mario Amaya, wounding him slightly.

A few hours later, she surrendered to a young traffic cop in Times Square. Once in custody, she explained, "It's not often I shoot somebody. I didn't do it for nothing. Warhol had me tied up lock, stock and barrel. He was going to do something to me which would have ruined me." The *New York Post* quoted her on her motive for the shooting: "I have a lot of very involved reasons. Read my manifesto and it will tell you what I am."

During the hearing on June 5, she refused the service of two lawyers that Girodias had hired for her. Valerie was placed in the prison ward of Elmhurst Psychiatric Hospital, and referred for psychological evaluation to Dr. Ruth Cooper. Over twenty years later, Valerie is a surprisingly vivid memory for Dr. Cooper, who remembered her with sympathy as an "engaging young woman—challenging and stimulating," with a sense of humor, who was obsessed with gender and would continuously turn the conversation back to the inferiority of the male.

Valerie was given the full battery of tests. She was asked to make "projective drawings," in which she created "a female who, except for her flowing hair, is an extremely phallic, aggressive creature, far more masculine than the male." The report went on to say that "though she makes strenuous efforts to present herself as a hard, tough, cynical misanthrope, Miss Solanas is actually a very frightened and depressed child. . . . When the examiner tentatively verbalized awareness of Miss Solanas' depression and anxiety, there was a marked startled reaction on Miss Solanas' part. She made a feeble effort to deny the observation but was clearly very close to tears."

Valerie's problems, the psychiatrist concluded, came from rejection by her mother, who was more interested in men: "While she has consciously devoted much of her energy to proving what 'pigs' and 'exploiters' men were, her unconscious strivings have been to be a male and thus, perhaps, to win her mother's love." She was a victim of sexual confusion, Dr. Cooper decided; politics were not mentioned. "The diagnostic impression is of a Schizophrenic Reaction, paranoid type with marked depression and potential for acting out."

On Christmas Day, Warhol answered the phone. It was Valerie: "I want you to drop all criminal charges, pay twenty thousand dollars for my manuscripts, put me in more movies and get me booked on Johnny Carson. If you don't, I can always do it again."

To Maurice Girodias, she wrote that "I know Warhol has front groups, that he's an invisible partner in a lot of enterprises. . . . My next book will be called "Why I Shot Andy Warhol &

Other Chit Chat." She kept up a lengthy correspondence with Girodias, who tried to arrange lawyers for her (she refused them), and who even went to visit her in prison, where she seemed "totally unconcerned, unaware, uninterested in her own or anyone else's feelings." When he asked, "If you are ever released, will you come shoot me?" she replied, "You? Oh, no! And I'm over it now, in any case; I don't have to do it again."

Girodias had no fear of Valerie, which is surprising because several sources suggest that he was her first target. Jeffrey LeGear wrote to Warhol, "I'm not sure if Valerie would have shot you if Girodias had been as well known as you are." On the morning of June 3, she had gone to the Olympia Press offices in Gramercy Park, where she found that Girodias was in Montreal; she went on to the Factory. But would Valerie really have shot Girodias? He had a better sense of how to handle her. He at least dealt with her directly, face-to-face, giving her the attention she craved, where Warhol ignored her, exacerbating the pain of a lifetime of rejection.

Certainly, Girodias had an ulterior motive for his attentions. He was thrilled that the shooting provided a wonderful publishing opportunity for the *Manifesto*. He prepared an edition of the *Manifesto* whose back cover reproduced the front page of the *New York Post* with the headline ANDY WARHOL FIGHTS FOR LIFE.

In Girodias's foreword to his edition of the *Manifesto*, he says, "This little book is my contribution to the study of violence," as if it were a pathological study of an assassin. Through a friend, Valerie complained, "Why did you not have the guts . . . to let the *Manifesto* stand or fall on its own? Why were you so cowardly as to try and explain it away even before it had a chance to speak for itself? Was there ever an author who was attacked and put down by her own editor and publisher, and right in her own book too?"

Valerie bombarded Girodias with furious letters that mixed threats with childlike pleas for attention. However, as comedy was second nature to her, even her hate letters had a satiric edge:

you must strive to transcend your sniveling self & immerse yourself in the betterment of the community; you must learn to pretend you're human, & not a toad, become an expert human impersonator. You must have as your sole goal the happiness of women, both in the mass and those you're personally associated with. I'm convinced that the rewards you reap from doing so will be enormous. . . .

As for your lawyer proposal, forget it—I'll *never* give in to it.

Would you like to interview me?

WARHOL GUN GIRL GETS THREE YEARS

Valerie had been lucky enough to go up before Judge Culkin, who was known for light sentencing. When Valerie's case came up for parole, Assistant District Attorney Lankler, who had handled the case, wrote this recommendation: "After almost killing the victim of this case; after being sent to Matteawan; after pleading guilty to Assault 1 this defendant received this outrageously low sentence. She should serve every day of it."

Jeremiah Newton stated his belief that spiritually, at least, [Valerie and Warhol] "both died the moment she shot him." Warhol never recovered the sense of invulnerability that had fueled him as an artist. As for Valerie, she was now "the crazy woman who shot Andy Warhol." She would never have what she most wanted: to be taken seriously as a writer.

There were many sightings of Valerie Solanas in the East Village in the late seventies, sleeping on a bench in Thompson Square Park or sitting on a stoop on St. Mark's Place, dirty and unkempt, like a dazed street person. And yet it was at this time that she managed to print a new edition of her *Manifesto,* and wrote this sparkling advertisement:

Olympia Press went bankrupt and the publishing rights to SCUM Manifesto reverted to me, Valerie Solanas,

so I'm issuing the CORRECT edition, MY edition of
SCUM Manifesto. . . . I'll let anybody who wants to
hawk it—women, men, Hare Krishna; Daughter of the
American Revolution, the American Legion. Maurice
Girodias, you're always in financial straits. Here's your
big chance—hawk SCUM Manifesto. You can peddle
it around the massage parlor district. Anita Bryant,
finance your anti-fag campaign selling the only book
worth selling—SCUM Manifesto. Andy Warhol,
peddle it at all those hot shit parties you go to . . .
Minimum orders for peddlers is 200. No credit, no
discounts. I don't like arithmetic. And don't have gang
wars over territories—that's not nice.

In 1985, Andy Warhol was interviewed by the British style
magazine the *Face*. When asked what would happen to his collection when he died, he replied, "I'm dead already." On Febru-
ary 22, 1987, a trip to New York Hospital achieved what Valerie
had failed to do. As if their lives were still connected, she died a
year later. With the bad timing and bad luck that dogged her life,
she probably never knew about the resurgence of interest in her
Manifesto.

Valerie never knew that we wanted to make a film about
her. I feel bitter on her behalf that she can never experience her
newfound celebrity, and I also know how impossible it would have
been to make this film if she were still alive. The Valerie Solanas
of *I Shot Andy Warhol* may be based on research, but it is also the
Valerie that I and the researcher Diane Tucker and the writer
Daniel Minahan and the actress Lili Taylor created in our heads.
If there was one thing Valerie hated, it was loss of control.

When it came time to write this screenplay, my co-writer
Daniel Minahan was enormously influential in creating the film's
tone and style and structure, and in providing visual ideas and
witty dialogue. It was Dan who gently drew me away from obsessive clinging to the facts, who showed me there were imagina-

tive ways to move the plot forward, and that I would not be shot at dawn for making something up. He suggested, for instance, that Valerie should meet Girodias while she is trying to sell him conversation rather than simply running into him in the Chelsea Hotel.

As far as we know, there was never a rehearsal of "Up Your Ass" at Nedick's, and Candy didn't bring Valerie to the Factory or watch the Miss America pageant with her, which happened after the shooting. We don't even know if Valerie went to a party at the Factory, although it seems likely she did. Other scenes, which probably seem made up, are true. She did sleep with a member of Up against the Wall Motherfucker (although that's not where she got the gun), and he did stage a piece of street theater on her behalf and recite a poem. That street theater scene, which is in the screenplay, is the one I regret most having to cut from the final film.

We began filming *I Shot Andy Warhol* in the spring of 1995. Just before preproduction started, I made a pilgrimage to San Francisco to visit the address where Valerie's body was found. Fifty-six Mason Street turned out to be a cavernous welfare hotel, with worn linoleum and scrawled signs warning tenants about loud radios and paying the rent on time. It was in the worst part of the Tenderloin, near a couple of theaters that show pornographic films; evidently, Valerie's circumstances had never changed.

On April 25, 1988, the super used a pass key to unlock her room because she had not been seen for a week, and the rent was overdue. The police report states that the "victim was found kneeling on the floor of the one room apt., and her upper torso was facing down on the side of the bed. Her body was covered with maggots and the room appeared orderly."

The coroner listed the cause of death as bronchopneumonia brought on by emphysema. A different super was on duty the day

I went there, but he had a vague memory of Valerie. Once, he had to enter her room, and he saw her typing at her desk. There was a pile of typewritten pages beside her. What she was writing and what happened to the manuscript remain a mystery.

New York
May 1996

I Shot Andy Warhol

Mary Harron

and

Daniel Minahan

Cast

Valerie Solanas	Lili Taylor
Andy Warhol	Jared Harris
Fred Hughes	Craig Chester
Mario Amaya	Massimo Audiello
Danny	Victor Browne
Louis Solanas	Mark Margolis
Waitress	Dawn Didawick
Mrs. Warhola	Faith Geer
Viva	Tahnee Welch
Iris	Anna Thomson
Billy Name	James Lyons
Gerard	Donovan Leitch
Detective Lankler	Jeff Webster
Psychiatrist	Lola Pashalinski
First Reporter	Henry Cabot Beck
Second Reporter	Christopher Cook
Editor of Paper	Edoardo Ballerini
Clean-cut Boy	Gabriel Mick
Jean	Marian Quinn
Candy Darling	Stephen Dorff
Stevie	Martha Plimpton
Wheelchair Concierge	Lynn Cohen
Passerby	Bill Lin
Squat Man	John Ventemiglia
Maitre D'	Stan Tracy
Paul Morrissey	Reg Rogers
Brigid	Coco McPherson

Susan	Lorraine Farris
Rotten Rita	Billy Erb
Maurice Girodias	Lothaire Bluteau
Old Man	Fenton Lawless
Marilyn	Laura Ekstrand
Laura	Jill Hennessy
Manager, Nedick's	Michelle Hurst
Jackie Curtis	Jamie Harold
Ondine	Michael Imperioli
Jeremiah	Danny Morgenstern
Comtesse de Courcy	Anh Duong
Isabelle de Courcy	Caroline Benezet-Brown
Manager, Chelsea Hotel	Michael Stumm
Tom	Bill Sage
Police Chief	Steve Itkin
Ultra Violet	Myriam Cyr
Revolutionary	Eric Mabius
Girl Panhandler	Debbon Ayer
Mark Motherfucker	Justin Theroux
Disinterested Girl	Anna Grace
Alison	Isabel Gillies
Alan Burke	Peter Friedman
Director	Davis Hall
Cecil the Pornographer	Daniel Haughey
A-Head	Kevin Rendon
The Party Band	Georgia Hubley
	Ira Kaplan
	James McNew
	Tara Key

Crew

Executive Producers	Lindsay Law
	Anthony Wall
Director and Writer	Mary Harron
Co-Writer	Daniel Minahan
Producers	Tom Kalin
	Christine Vachon
Original Score	John Cale
Music Supervisor	Randall Poster
Line Producer	Pamela Koffler
Unit Production Manager	Blair Breard
Production Coordinator	Eva Kolodner
Assistant Production Coordinator	Katie Roumel
Assistant to the Producers	John Leonard
Assistant to the Director	Linzy Emery
First Assistant Director	Jeffrey Lazar
Second Assistant Director	Jody Solomon
Second Second Assistant Director	John Tyson
Locations Manager	Tom Whelan
Assistant Locations Manager	Andy Clark
Director of Photography	Ellen Kuras
First Assistant Camera	Susanna Virtanen
Second Assistant Camera	Danya Reich
Camera P.A.	Kenji Tanaka
Script Supervisor	Sheila G. Waldron
Additional Camera Operator	Stephen Kazmierski
Additional First Assistant	Axel Bauman

Stills Photographer	Bill Foley
Special Photography	Joyce George
Additional Stills	Nan Goldin
	Christopher Smith
	Christopher Makos
Gaffer	John Nadeau
Best Boy Electric	Simone Perusse
Third Electric	Antonio Rossi
Key Grip	Danny Beaman
Best Boy Grip	Toshiaki Ozawa
Third Grip	James Ferris
Sound Mixer	Robert Larrea
Boom Operator	Jeannie Gilliland
Production Designer	Thérèse DePrez
Art Department Coordinator	John Bruce
Visual Consultant	Diane Lederman
Art Department Researcher	Gideon Ponté
Art Assistant	John Oglevee
Silk Screener	Jill Nichols
Property Master	Annie Ballard
Assistant Props	Sarah Lavery
Set Dresser	Victoria Krasnakevich
Assistant Decorator	Dina Goldman
Costume Designer	David Robinson
Assistant Costume Designer	Joan Kaufman
Wardrobe Supervisor	Wendy Van Dyke
Key Hair Stylist	Edward St. George
Key Makeup Artist	Judy Chin
Special Effects Makeup	Rob Benevides
Editor	Keith Reamer
Associate Editor	Merril Stern
Supervising Sound Editor	Harry Peck Bolles
Sound Editor	Kevin Lee
ADR Editor	Harriet Fidlow
Music Editor	James Flatto

Casting	Hopkins, Smith & Barden
Extras Casting	Karen Etkoff and Bill Butler
Production Publicist	David Kirby
Publicist	Clein and White
Production Assistants	Nancy Kolomitz
	Susan Perlman
	René Veilleux

INTERIOR: THE NEW FACTORY. DAY.

A series of tableaux, showing the aftermath of the shooting. These should be like police photos: very stark, shot from above, and with just the faintest tremor of movement to show they are *not* stills: An overturned telephone, the tangled wires spattered with blood.
A floor covered with glittering fragments of broken glass; two legs twitching under a desk.
A close-up of a hand clutching a door handle, desperately pulling it closed as someone tries to open it on the other side.
An abandoned editing table with a reel of film whirring round and round.
In a distant corner of the Factory, MARIO AMAYA, a man in a white suit, shot in the buttock, struggles to crawl across the floor.
An extreme close-up of the barrel of a gun pointed at the camera.
FRED HUGHES kneels on the ground, looking into the camera. The reverse angle: FRED with his back to us in the foreground; VALERIE SOLANAS in the background by the elevator.
The elevator doors open behind her.

> FRED
> (*obviously terrified and trying to sound calm*)
> There's the elevator, Valerie. *The elevator.* Just take it.

Cut to Valerie's point of view as she backs into the elevator. For a moment, we see a panorama of the whole scene—shattered glass, FRED kneeling, ANDY WARHOL under a desk, AMAYA crawling in the distance. BILLY NAME and DANNY are present. The elevator doors close.

INTERIOR: NEW JERSEY BAR-RESTAURANT. DAY.

The swinging doors of the kitchen open as a middle-aged man in a white apron struggles in, carrying a crate of bottles. He sets it down with a crash.

> WOMAN
> (*offscreen*)
> Louis, come here quick! I think your daughter's on TV!

Holding a tray, a WAITRESS stands motionless, staring at the television set over the bar.
The television is playing footage of Valerie's arrest. As she is led into the station, VALERIE turns to the camera and smiles.

> WAITRESS
> Isn't that Valerie?

Rear view of LOUIS SOLANAS and the WAITRESS silhouetted against the television as they watch the news reports giving the rundown on Warhol.
Absentmindedly, the WAITRESS picks a french fry from the plate she is carrying and eats it as she watches the screen.
On the television screen, the POLICE CHIEF is briefing reporters:

> POLICE CHIEF
> At exactly 4:30 P.M. this day, at 33 Union Square West, two males were shot by a female. One of them was Andy Warhol, who was the owner of Warhol Films located at this location, and the second was Mario Amaya.

Cut back to LOUIS staring at the television screen.

> LOUIS
> Jesus Christ, now she's shot somebody.

INTERIOR: CATHOLIC HOSPITAL. LOBBY.

Chaos. In one corner, MRS. WARHOLA, an old lady in a babushka, is rocking back and forth, weeping, "What have they done to me, Andy?" and being comforted by VIVA. In another corner, SUPER-STAR NUMBER ONE is holding forth to the press.

> SUPERSTAR NUMBER ONE
> I always thought Andy was a great artist. He made three films with me. My most recent role was in *I, a Man*, where I lie on the floor naked while discussing the philosophy of love . . .

One group of Warhol's friends stands under a statue of the Virgin Mary, while another sits on a bench beneath a painting of the sacred heart. Others are camped out on the floor eating sandwiches, waiting for news. People are weeping; someone is reciting a poem.

> MRS. WARHOLA
> (*weeping, rocking back and forth*)
> Andy's a good boy. He go twelve o'clock mass Saint Paul's . . .

> SUPERSTAR NUMBER ONE
> (*addressing a reporter*)
> Violence is everywhere in the air today. Andy got hurt in the big game of reality . . .

The double doors burst open, and a burly POLICEMAN strides in. He is holding something gingerly in one hand, keeping it at arm's length; he seems to be carrying a small silver dog by the scruff of its neck.

> POLICEMAN
>
> Can you take this?

> RECEPTIONIST NUN
>
> What *is* it?

Wordlessly, the POLICEMAN puts it down on the desk. The RECEPTIONIST NUN stares at it, repulsed. It is Warhol's silver wig.

INTERIOR: POLICE INTERROGATION ROOM. NIGHT.

The assistant district attorney, LANKLER, is questioning VALERIE, who slumps in her chair. She is in a pool of light, with the rest of the room only dimly visible.

> LANKLER
>
> You are Valerie Jean Solanas?

> VALERIE
>
> Solanas. That's right.

> LANKLER
>
> And where do you live?

> VALERIE
>
> Nowhere.

> LANKLER
>
> Where do you come from?

> VALERIE
>
> The river.

FLASHBACK: EXTERIOR: ATLANTIC CITY. DAY.

Super-8, like a home movie.

The New Jersey shore. The sound of the ocean and, in the distance, children's voices.

A street of little frame houses right next to the boardwalk. A group of children playing in the street. VALERIE, a tall, thin twelve-year-old with bushy hair, is among them.

Two plump little girls—one of them Valerie's blond younger sister—sit on a wall, watching. They are wearing frilly bathing suits. An older boy hits one of the little girls. VALERIE knocks him to the ground and beats the shit out of him.

INTERIOR: POLICE INTERROGATION ROOM. NIGHT.

This time we see the whole room. There are three men, with their backs to us, in a semicircle facing VALERIE: LANKLER, a police officer, and a male clerk, who sits in the background, taking down the interrogation.

The contents of Valerie's bag—including two guns and an ice pick—are on a tray on the desk in front of them, with identification labels marking each object.

LANKLER is being quite gentle with VALERIE: this is a deposition, not an interrogation. She is calm, subdued, slightly disoriented.

> LANKLER
>
> Miss Solanas, you don't have to answer any of my questions if you don't want to. Do you understand that?
>
> VALERIE
>
> Hm mm.

> LANKLER
>
> Instead of saying "hm mm," because he's got to take it down on the machine, could you say either "yes" or "no"?

> VALERIE

Yes.

> LANKLER

All right. Now, knowing what your rights are, knowing that I'd like to ask you some questions about what happened this afternoon, do you want to tell me what happened?

> VALERIE

Yes.

> LANKLER

You tell me in your own words what happened.

> VALERIE

Very simply. I shot him.

> LANKLER

Who did you shoot?

> VALERIE

Andy Warhol.

> LANKLER

What did you shoot him with?

> VALERIE

A gun.

> LANKLER

That gun?

> VALERIE

Yeah. Thirty-two-caliber Beretta.

LANKLER

Why did you want to shoot Andy Warhol?

VALERIE

That's something—it's very involved, and I don't want to get into that right now.

LANKLER

You don't have to get into anything if you don't want to. Do you know what part of his body you shot him?

VALERIE

According to the papers, it was a chest wound. Naturally, I was, like, sort of to the side, and I thought I was shooting from you know, like, from here.
(VALERIE *indicates*.)

Super-8: A flash of Valerie's hand carefully slipping the gun under Warhol's arm and pulling the trigger.

LANKLER

What did you need an ice pick for?

A pause as they all stare at the ice pick.

VALERIE

Actually, I had been carrying that on me for several days, and I didn't intend to use that one. I brought it with me. I had all my things in a bag, including the ice pick, which I had forgotten.

Pause.

LANKLER

Why did you shoot Andy Warhol?

> VALERIE
> I told you, I don't want to get into that.

INTERIOR: NEW JERSEY BAR-RESTAURANT. DAY.

Behind the bar, the WAITRESS hands the telephone to LOUIS.

> WAITRESS
> It's a woman; she's from the *New York Times*!

> LOUIS
> (*takes the receiver*)
> What can I do for you? . . . Look, I'm a bartender. I
> don't answer questions. I just listen to the other
> person. I'm a good listener . . . when was the last
> time I saw my daughter? I don't remember. Sorry.

LOUIS slams the receiver down.

FLASHBACK.

Close-up of twelve-year-old VALERIE looking straight into the camera—like a Warhol filmed portrait but in color Super-8 and from a high angle, as if she is looking up at someone. She has no particular expression on her face.

> PSYCHIATRIST
> (*voice-over*)
> The patient is a twenty-eight-year-old single woman
> who was admitted to this hospital on June fifth. She
> was born and raised in Atlantic City, New Jersey.

Wide shot of a row of tract houses, right under the boardwalk.

PSYCHIATRIST
(*voice-over*)
She describes a rather pitiful childhood, including parental conflict, sexual molestation by her father, and separation from her home.

INTERIOR: PSYCHIATRIST'S OFFICE, ELMHURST HOSPITAL. DAY.

The assistant district attorney, LANKLER, sits facing a female PSY-CHIATRIST, a gray-haired woman in her fifties. Her manner is kindly but austere, and there is something nunlike about her. She refers to her notes occasionally as she delivers her report.

PSYCHIATRIST
By the age of thirteen, she had many sexual experiences. It was about this time her mother remarried for the second time. At age fourteen, she was sent to a boarding school, where she stayed for about two years. It was here that she had her first homosexual experiences.

EXTERIOR: POLICE STATION. NIGHT.

PSYCHIATRIST
(*voice-over*)
At age sixteen, she returned home. Her schoolwork improved, and it was noted that she seemed to possess exceptional intellectual ability.

Her deposition over, VALERIE is led out through the station doors by a female detective. VALERIE has her hands tied behind her back. She is immediately surrounded by reporters, their flashbulbs popping.

> FIRST REPORTER
> This way, Valerie!

VALERIE turns her head for the camera, and the flashbulb pops.

> SECOND REPORTER
> This way, honey.

Another flashbulb pops.
Another reporter shouts from the crowd.

> FIRST REPORTER
> Where did you get the gun?

> VALERIE
> (*smiling graciously, obviously enjoying the attention*)
> In Vermont.

> FIRST REPORTER
> Why did you shoot Andy Warhol?

> VALERIE
> I have a lot of very involved reasons. Read my mani-
> festo, and it will tell you what I am.

INTERIOR: PSYCHIATRIST'S OFFICE, ELMHURST HOSPITAL. DAY.
Closeup of "SCUM Manifesto" on Lankler's desk.

> LANKLER
> Have you copies of any of the school reports?

> PSYCHIATRIST
> (*hands* LANKLER *a letter*)

I have this. In 1958, her high school principal wrote
a letter on her behalf . . .

LANKLER
(*takes it and begins to read it aloud to himself*)
I understand that Valerie Solanas needs a letter of
recommendation.

EXTERIOR: POLICE STATION. NIGHT.

A crash of noise: sirens, traffic, people shouting. The street sounds
die away and are replaced by a voice-over of LANKLER reading the
principal's letter:

LANKLER
(*voice-over*)
She has proved to be an exceptionally bright girl with
lots of courage and determination.

VALERIE is hustled through the crowd to a waiting police car.

LANKLER
(*voice-over continues*)
Valerie is a highly responsible and dependable person, well suited to the study of psychology at university level.

INTERIOR: LABORATORY. NIGHT.

Scene dissolves to a medical laboratory. Wide shot, lots of tables.
VALERIE is in the middle of the room, alone at night, in a pool of
light. She is doing something to rats.

LANKLER
(*voice-over*)

She possesses much initiative and always meets her
obstacles by setting new goals . . .

Close in on VALERIE. She holds up a rat, wriggling in the light
and inspects its tiny genitalia.

> VALERIE
> (*voice-over*)
> The male is a biological accident: the *y*, male, gene
> is an incomplete *x* or female gene; that is, has an
> incomplete set of chromosomes. It is now technically
> possible to reproduce without the aid of males and
> to produce only females.
> (*She smiles at the rat as she places it in a box.*)
> We must begin immediately to do so . . .

INTERIOR: STUDENT NEWSPAPER OFFICE. DAY.

A large, open room crammed with desks and typewriters. The
students are clean cut and perky, with the curiously middle-aged
look of college students of the 1950s. The girls are wearing plaid
skirts, sweaters, pearls, little white blouses with Peter Pan collars.
The boys have crew cuts and sports jackets. They are meeting a
production deadline, and there is a busy hum of activity, with
students carrying piles of copy back and forth.

In one corner of the room, the EDITOR is dictating this week's
editorial to his FEMALE ASSISTANT:

> EDITOR
> On the subject of vandalism on campus. We're told
> that one hundred ashtrays have disappeared from the
> student union since its opening . . .

The speech becomes a voice-over for shots of wholesome young
people working around the office.

> EDITOR
> (*voice-over*)
> Last Saturday, following the pep rally, someone unscrewed all the mirrors in the men's room and would have taken the mirrors had they not been screwed to the wall . . .

Cut to an ashtray piled high with cigarette butts.
Cut to VALERIE slouching in a chair. She is smoking as she reads through a pile of letters, carefully writing something on each one and putting them in envelopes. She looks startlingly butch compared to the other girls in the room, with her cropped hair, dungarees, and a man's shirt. She radiates hostility, even in repose. A CLEAN-CUT BOY in a crew cut and glasses is sitting opposite her, also going through the letters.

> CLEAN-CUT BOY
> Listen to this. It's from the head of Sigma Delta Chi:

> Dear Editor,
> Is a corsage appropriate only at class formals, or should one be worn at more casual affairs? I think it would be helpful to all students if the university adopted a definite policy on the corsage issue.

> VALERIE
> (*deadpan*)
> An earth-shattering dilemma.

The CLEAN-CUT BOY stares back at VALERIE earnestly. He sees nothing funny in this.

> CLEAN-CUT BOY
> (*handing her the letter*)
> It's a tricky one. Do you want to answer it?

VALERIE
(*busy writing*)
Sure.

Cut to view over Valerie's shoulder. She has written FUCK YOU in huge letters over the letter and is about to put it back in an envelope addressed to the sorority.

INTERIOR: COLLEGE DORMITORY STUDY ROOM. DAY.

VALERIE and JEAN—a pretty, dark-haired student—are seated opposite each other at a desk in their dormitory study room.

JEAN
(*shuffling through papers*)
Thanks for doing this with me, Val. Now, remember, just say the first word that comes into your mind.

VALERIE
(*pulling on a cigarette*)
Okay.

JEAN
Lamp.

VALERIE
Shade.

JEAN
Hat.

VALERIE
Cap.

JEAN
Mountain.

VALERIE
Hill.

JEAN
Suicide.

VALERIE
Kill.

Cut to the view below the table.
As JEAN continues to ask questions, VALERIE begins rubbing her leg against Jean's under the table.

JEAN
Black.

VALERIE
White.

JEAN
Love.

VALERIE
Hate.

JEAN
Boyfriend.

VALERIE
Girlfriend.

Nervously, JEAN withdraws her leg.

> JEAN
> Maybe we should stop there. Bill's coming to pick
> me up.

INTERIOR: STAIRCASE, COLLEGE DORMITORY. DAY.

VALERIE stands at the top of a long staircase, white faced and shaking. She heaves a case of empty Coke bottles down the stairs at JEAN. The bottles smash at the bottom of the stairs, as VALERIE screams insults at JEAN as the frightened girl backs away.

INTERIOR: PSYCHIATRIST'S OFFICE, ELMHURST HOSPITAL. DAY.

The PSYCHIATRIST continues to read to LANKLER from her report.

> PSYCHIATRIST
> Miss Solanas entered the University of Maryland in
> 1958 and completely supported herself during the
> next four years—

EXTERIOR: LAWN GRADUATION CEREMONY. DAY.

> PSYCHIATRIST
> (*voice-over*)
> During which time she earned As in her major of
> psychology.

VALERIE in her graduation gown stands in line to receive her degree. She is smoking a cigarette, which she tries to hide behind her hand.

INTERIOR: CHEAP HOTEL ROOM, ATLANTIC CITY. DAY.

> PSYCHIATRIST
> (*voice-over*)
> Her college stay was also stormy in that she was in
> frequent disciplinary difficulty and on one occasion
> was almost expelled.

A man is sprawled facedown on the bed, with his trousers around his knees, drunkenly snoring. VALERIE is very carefully and quietly going through the pockets of his jacket, which is hanging on a chair. This is the first time we see her wearing makeup, which is somewhat smeared.

EXTERIOR: LAWN GRADUATION CEREMONY. DAY.

> PSYCHIATRIST
> (*voice-over*)
> During the summers of her third and fourth college
> year, she made money by prostitution while living a
> "homosexual life for enjoyment."

A close-up of VALERIE receiving her degree from the CHANCELLOR, smiling triumphantly.

INTERIOR: CHEAP HOTEL ROOM, ATLANTIC CITY. DAY.

> PSYCHIATRIST
> (*voice-over*)

In 1963, she went to Minnesota to do her graduate
work in psychology. During the first year, she says,
she got bored and never returned.

Stuffing the money from the man's wallet into her coat pocket,
VALERIE glides to the door and closes it behind her.

INTERIOR: PSYCHIATRIST'S OFFICE, ELMHURST HOSPITAL. DAY.

The PSYCHIATRIST continues to read from her report to LANKLER.

> PSYCHIATRIST
> She tells us for the last five years she "knocked
> around" and lived with several men, none of whom
> she liked . . .
> For many years, the patient has been developing an
> interest in the "natural superiority of women over
> men." Within the past three to four years, she de-
> cided to put her thoughts on paper . . .

Close-up of pamphlet on Lankler's desk. Camera tracks along the
words: SCUM (Society for Cutting up Men) MANIFESTO.

MANIFESTO SEQUENCE.

The manifesto readings will always be shot in black and white.
The setting should be formal but abstract: VALERIE is standing
against a white wall, with the manifesto in her hand. This setting
is based on Warhol's film screen tests. There should be something
idealizing about the lighting—VALERIE is in film heaven, talking
to us.
VALERIE will refer to the manifesto occasionally, but generally, she
speaks from memory. The tone of these readings is ironic, controlled, logical, articulate. There should be an intensity about
them, but nothing strident or overemotional.

VALERIE

Life in this society being, at best, an utter bore and
no aspect of society being at all relevant to women,
there remains to civic-minded, responsible, thrill-
seeking females only to overthrow the government,
eliminate the money system, institute complete automation, and destroy the male sex.

EXTERIOR: WASHINGTON SQUARE. NIGHT.

Title on-screen: SUMMER 1966.
VALERIE approaches the park. A group of drag queens are hanging out, laughing, screaming, drinking, under a street lamp—an
island of light in the middle of the park. The lighting should be
unnatural; this is like a vision. We see VALERIE some distance away,
sitting on a bench in the dark, staring at them, fascinated.

EXTERIOR: NEW YORK ROOFTOP. EARLY MORNING.

Shots of the city in the early morning light. We find VALERIE sleeping on a rooftop, huddled in a sleeping bag.

EXTERIOR: WASHINGTON SQUARE PARK. DAY.

VALERIE is walking with STEVIE, a butch dyke. VALERIE is wearing a
pea coat, jeans, and a navy blue sailor's cap. Unless otherwise indi-
cated, she wears this cap in every scene from now on. As they walk
around the perimeter of the park, the camera follows, almost as
if it were a surveillance operation, picking up their conversation.

STEVIE

I'm sick of turning tricks. Money, I *hate* it. Why do
we have to need money?

> VALERIE

I need money, so I can get a room somewhere. I'm
sick of sleeping on rooftops. Hey, Stevie, can't I stay
with you?

> STEVIE

Are you kidding? My girlfriend would kill you.

> VALERIE

Yeah, you're right . . . oh, Jesus, what shit we have
to go through just to survive.

Suddenly, the camera halts. In front of them, they see a young
boyish-looking woman posed dramatically on the other side of
the railings. She is wearing narrow black trousers, a white blouse,
a shabby black jacket. Her dark hair is shoulder length, and she is
wearing white lipstick, eyeliner, and mascara.

> STEVIE

Hi, Jimmy. Valerie, this is Jimmy. Jimmy, Valerie.

> CANDY
> (*offended*)

I'm called Candy now.

> VALERIE
> (*astonished*)

You're a guy? God—I thought you were a lesbian.

> CANDY
> (*tossing her hair*)

Thank you. A lot of people think that. May I have a
cigarette?

VALERIE passes her one through the railings. CANDY takes it, and
VALERIE gives her a light.

CANDY strikes a pose as she draws on her cigarette and nods thank you.

> VALERIE
>
> So do you live 'round here?

> CANDY
> (*striking a pose*)
>
> Who lives?
> (*She drops the pose.*)
> Natalie Wood—*Rebel without a Cause.*

CANDY's speech is always stylized—she talks a little like Marilyn Monroe—the product of many years spent studying Hollywood glamour queens. She slips effortlessly in and out of parodies of movies or television commercials.

> VALERIE
>
> I need a room.

CANDY takes another drag on her cigarette.

> CANDY
>
> Try the Hotel Earle . . . comfort and convenience for the modern girl.

Dissolve on a close-up of Candy's face as she takes another drag and blows smoke at the camera.

INTERIOR: HOTEL EARLE LOBBY. NIGHT.

A squalid flophouse. A malevolent CONCIERGE guards from the reception area in case the guests bring in visitors unworthy of the hotel's reputation. The CONCIERGE darts about in a wheelchair be-cause—in keeping with the hotel's general ambience—she has no legs.

A group of drag queens, including CANDY, burst in the door, with VALERIE in tow. They run up the stairs as the CONCIERGE shouts insults after them:

> CONCIERGE
> No visitors after ten o'clock! Come back, you whores!

CANDY leans over the banister.

> CANDY
> (*sweetly*)
> Aren't you going to run after us?

> CONCIERGE
> How dare you—that's a terrible thing to say!

> CANDY
> Honey, it's a terrible world.

The drag queens and VALERIE run up the stairs, laughing.

INTERIOR: HOTEL EARLE CORRIDOR. A FEW DAYS LATER.

Wide shot of the corridor of the Hotel Earle's drag queen–lesbian wing.
A boy in a kimono, clutching something to his breast, runs from one room to an open door across the hall, screaming with laughter, and slams the door behind him. A voice screams from across the hall:

> DRAG QUEEN
> (*offscreen*)
> Bring that cologne back, Mary, or I'll tear your nelly head off!!

Another door opens, and a deep woman's voice screams from inside:

> WOMAN
> (*offscreen*)
> Don't you fairies ever shut up?!

The door slams shut.
Cut to the door to Candy's room. It is decorated with a big, homemade gold star.

INTERIOR: CANDY'S ROOM, HOTEL EARLE. DAY.

A squalid room, with a hot plate and a pathetic collection of dishes: two chipped plates, two forks, one knife, several bent spoons, and some glasses stolen from a bar. There are a few thrift-shop dresses in the closet and a pile of old movie and fashion magazines on the floor. Candy's prized collection of makeup is laid out on the dressing table. A box of Kotex is prominently displayed on the dresser.

CANDY is lying on the bed, wrapped in an old Chinese kimono, writing her diary. As she writes, she addresses the empty room:

> CANDY
> Dear Diary,
> I try to get what I want whenever it's possible . . .
> (*pause*)
> I have always found that socially unacceptable people
> make the best lovers because they are more sensitive.

In neat capitals, she writes in her notebook: TRICKY MOTHER NATURE.

> I can be happy and fulfilled—I will never doubt it. I
> cannot afford to. Each thought, each movement
> tuned to some great moving force.

The sound of typing, emanating from the next room, floats over the last few lines.

INTERIOR: VALERIE'S ROOM, HOTEL EARLE. DAY.

Valerie's room is identical to Candy's but with a battered typewriter set up instead of a vanity, and it is extremely messy. The bed is unmade, and piles of manuscript cover every surface. She is sitting at a desk, hammering away at the typewriter. Close-ups of her hands on the keys and the words being typed out. The desk is rickety and everything shakes as she types.

> VALERIE
> (*voice-over*)
> A Young Girl's Primer, or How to Attain the Leisure Class, by Valerie Solanas.
> Being fresh out of college, I found myself in the typically feminine dilemma of carving out for myself in a male world a way of life appropriate to a young woman of taste, cultivation, and sensitivity.

EXTERIOR: GREENWICH VILLAGE STREET. DAY.

> VALERIE
> (*voice-over*)
> There must be nothing crass—like work. However, a girl must survive. So, after a cool appraisal of the social scene, I finally hit upon an excellent paying occupation . . .

VALERIE saunters around a street corner in Sheridan Square. This scene and all the panhandling sequences have a theme music: a light upbeat sound with female voices, similar to Brazil 66. It should sound like the theme music for an early sixties movie about a young girl running around Manhattan, like *Breakfast at Tiffany's* or *That Girl*, but the images that accompany the music are not of a glamorous New York but a grubby bohemian downtown.

VALERIE stops a male PASSERBY.

Valerie's persona in the panhandling sequences is subtly different from the Valerie we have seen before. This is Valerie as she would most like to be: sharp, cool, and confident, with none of the insecurity she sometimes displays.

> VALERIE
> Pardon me, sir, do you have fifteen cents?

> PASSERBY
> No.

> VALERIE
> You gotta dime?

> PASSERBY
> No.

> VALERIE
> Nickel?

> PASSERBY
> NO!

> VALERIE
> Dollar bill?

> PASSERBY
> (*gives in*)
> Here, here's a quarter.

VALERIE pockets the quarter. A GIRL PANHANDLER approaches.

> GIRL PANHANDLER
> Hey, Val, you got a dime?

> VALERIE
> Beat it, you chiseling little bastard.

VALERIE sets off around the block again, accompanied by the theme music.

> VALERIE
> (*voice-over*)
> This job offers broad opportunities for travel—around and around the block. And to think—some girls settle for Europe.

INTERIOR: NEDICK'S RESTAURANT. NIGHT.

The entire restaurant is painted a once glowing, now faded orange. It is the hangout for an assortment of drag queens, junkies, and Village freaks, who feed off phallic-looking hot dogs and toxic-looking orange drinks. It is now 3 A.M., and the restaurant—with its ghostly strip lighting that gives everyone a weird, unhealthy glow—has the relaxed atmosphere of an after-hours club for outcasts only.

VALERIE and STEVIE are sitting at a table. VALERIE is in midmonologue; STEVIE is smoking cigarettes and stubbing them out in her plate and looking bored.

> VALERIE
> (*intensely*)
> The only way to take over is to get rid of the money system. And with females running the show, we won't need any kind of a government; it won't be necessary.

                              STEVIE
How do you know?

                              VALERIE
Well, I don't have any data to prove it—it's all infer-
ence from behavior—but I'm convinced I'm correct.

In the background, Chris Montez's "The More I See You" has
come on the jukebox.
In the middle of the room, CANDY gets up on a chair and starts
lip-synching to the song.
Candy's hair is now dyed blond. She is wearing a skirt under a
belted trench coat, fishnet stockings, and high heels, and is notice-
ably more feminine looking than when we first saw her.
VALERIE turns her head to look.

                              STEVIE
Don't pay any attention. It only encourages her.

                              VALERIE
                  (*launching back into her speech*)
So eventually, there'll be only females, but in the
meantime, there's a transition . . .

STEVIE yawns.

                              VALERIE
I'm talking too much, aren't I?

STEVIE makes a resigned gesture.

                              VALERIE
Sorry. I'll shut up.

VALERIE and STEVIE sit and watch the passing scene. In the background, CANDY is finishing her performance, vamping along a row of tables. Her model here is Rita Hayworth in *Gilda*.
In a booth near them, two girls are necking passionately.
STEVIE throws a bread roll at them. They look up, alarmed.

> STEVIE
> (*disgusted*)
> Can't you girls afford a hotel?

> VALERIE
> (*sad and envious*)
> I wish I could find somebody just to be with.

> STEVIE
> Why don't you then?

> VALERIE
> Oh, it's never going to happen. Women never want to be with me.

MANIFESTO SEQUENCE.

> VALERIE
> The male tries to convince himself and women that the female function is to bear and raise children; soothe, relax, and boost the male ego. When in actual fact, the female function is to groove, relate, love, be herself, discover, explore, invent, solve problems, crack jokes, make music. All with love. In other words, create a magic world.

EXTERIOR: GREENWICH VILLAGE NEWSSTAND. DAY.

Back on the usual street, usual music, VALERIE is standing by the newsstand, leafing through a porno magazine, looking bored. She stops a dark-haired, balding SQUAT MAN as he passes.

> VALERIE
> Pardon me, sir, do you have fifteen cents?

> SQUAT MAN
> I got a lot more than fifteen cents.

> VALERIE
> Swinging! Then you can buy me dinner.

EXTERIOR: RESTAURANT DOOR. DAY.

VALERIE pushes the SQUAT MAN into the nearest restaurant, where the MAITRE D' bars them at the door.

> MAITRE D'
> Sorry, we don't serve panhandlers in here.

> VALERIE
> Your loss, you fat asshole; I'm a big eater.

INTERIOR: CHINESE RESTAURANT. DAY.

VALERIE and the SQUAT MAN sit across from each other in a Chinese restaurant.
She studies the menu and makes a face.

> VALERIE
> Can't I get something more substantial?

VALERIE tosses the menu aside and grabs a passing CHINESE WAITER by the arm. He is carrying a tray loaded with dishes, but he bends over to listen.

> VALERIE
>
> Hey, have you got a steak?

The CHINESE WAITER nods.

> VALERIE
>
> That's what I want. You bring me a good steak. Well done. And french fries and a salad.

> CHINESE WAITER
> (*disentangling his arm*)
> I come back, miss. I come back for order.

> VALERIE
> (*shouting at the retreating* CHINESE WAITER)
> Make sure there are plenty of french fries.

> SQUAT MAN
>
> Are you a lesbian?

> VALERIE
> (*shoveling bread into her mouth*)
> Yeah?

> SQUAT MAN
>
> Tell me—what do you lesbians do?

> VALERIE
> (*leaning across the table, tempting him*)
> Would you like to find out?

SQUAT MAN
Yeah . . . yeah, that's something I'd like to see.

VALERIE
For twenty-five bucks apiece, I think I could arrange it.

MANIFESTO SEQUENCE.

VALERIE
Although completely physical, the male is unfit even for stud service. Even assuming mechanical proficiency, which few men have, he is, first of all, incapable of zestfully, lustfully, tearing off a piece . . .

INTERIOR: HOTEL EARLE. DAY.

VALERIE
(*voice-over*)
To call a man an animal is to flatter him; he's a machine, a walking dildo.

VALERIE and STEVIE entwined on the bed, miming sexual ecstasy. The SQUAT MAN is in a chair watching them, jerking off. This is shot in the flat, awkward style of a low-budget sixties porno film.

INTERIOR: SQUALID HOTEL ROOM. DAY.

Another hotel room, VALERIE lying prone under a large, rumpled, sweaty man. She has her jacket on but her pants off, and is trying to smoke a cigarette.

VALERIE
(*voice-over*)

Eaten up with guilt, shame, fears, and insecurities, and obtaining, if he's lucky, a barely perceptible physical feeling, the male is, nonetheless, obsessed with screwing . . .

INTERIOR: SQUALID HOTEL ROOM. DAY.

Low angle, VALERIE standing in front of the camera, feet spread apart—dressed in worn tennis shoes.
A man's pallid naked buttocks seen through Valerie's legs. He has a paper bag over his head. She holds a belt in one hand.

MANIFESTO SEQUENCE.

VALERIE looks into the camera.

VALERIE
(*continues*)

He'll swim a river of snot, wade nostril deep through a mile of vomit if he thinks there'll be a friendly pussy awaiting him. He'll screw a woman he despises, any snaggle-toothed hag, and, furthermore, pay for the opportunity.

INTERIOR: CHELSEA HOTEL CORRIDOR. SAME DAY.

VALERIE is shutting the door of the hotel room. As she shuts it, we see a man lying passed out on the bed.
She walks quickly down the stairs. As she reaches the landing, she sees brilliant white light shining from an open door into the darkened corridor.

BILLY NAME staggers out, wiping perspiration from his face and gasping.
He is followed by PAUL MORRISSEY. They walk down the corridor a few steps, complaining about the heat.

> BILLY
> *More* lights?

VALERIE approaches the open door. Inside, there is bright light, heat shimmer, smoke. This is a vision, like her first sight of the drag queens in the park: she's in the darkness; they're in the light. Inside the room, a group are making a movie, a scene from *Chelsea Girls*. We see BRIGID on the bed, with her naked back to us. Another girl crouches under the desk. The phone is ringing, but no one answers it. We see a camera, lights. Our camera holds a fixed position outside the open door; occasionally, someone wanders into the frame, obscuring our view.

> VALERIE
> (*whispering*)
> What is this?

> BILLY
> (*gently steering her away from a lighting fixture*)
> Don't go too close, honey; you'll get burned.

> VALERIE
> You making a movie?

> BILLY
> (*earnestly*)
> It's an Andy Warhol Production.

> VALERIE
> Which one is he?

BILLY
Oh, he's not here today.

Close on VALERIE in profile, silhouetted as she stares fascinated into the brilliantly lit doorway.

INTERIOR: CANDY'S ROOM, HOTEL EARLE. DAY.

Close on Candy's hand fiddling with the dark roots of her hair, which is now bleached platinum blond.

CANDY
(*looking straight into the camera*)
When I get home from a hard day at the studio, I want to keep my breath kissing sweet. Today I had Limburger cheese and bagels for breakfast, Gorgonzola dressing for lunch, and steak and onions for dinner—but he'll never know. Because I use Dentamint, my breath is always *kissing sweet.*

Pull out to reveal that CANDY is delivering her monologue into the mirror on her rickety dressing room table.
She looks back for applause from VALERIE and STEVIE, who are lying on Candy's bed, which is covered with old magazines.

CANDY
Marilyn Monroe: *The Seven Year Itch.*

VALERIE and STEVIE ignore her.

VALERIE
(*leafing through a magazine*)
What the fuck am I going to do? That legless wonder downstairs says she's going to throw me out.

STEVIE

Get a job.

VALERIE and STEVIE look at each other and burst out laughing at the absurdity of this idea. They continue flicking through the magazines.

CANDY is looking in the mirror as she now bravely and unflinchingly plucks her eyebrows. Her eyes are tearing slightly with the pain.

CANDY

Last night I was in Max's Kansas City—
(*Without turning her head, she shifts her eyes in the mirror to look at* STEVIE *and* VALERIE *to make sure they understand the significance of this.*)
—that's *the* chic hangout for the jet set of the world.
Roger Vadim was there with Jane Fonda. Andy
Warhol was there too.

She peers in the mirror, blots one eyelid carefully with a tissue, and turns round.

CANDY

How do I look? Revlon Natural Wonder eye shadow.

CANDY bats her eyes. STEVIE and VALERIE look at her blankly.

CANDY
(*sighing*)
As I was saying, Andy Warhol was there. He's a very
famous artist.

VALERIE

I know who he is. I'm writing a play, and I want him
to produce it.

CANDY
(*returning to plucking her eyebrows*)
Well, Andy just makes movies now. I did Kim Novak
for him, and he was very impressed. He invited me
to go to his studio—they call it the Factory. It's
where the in crowd go when they're not at Max's
Kansas City . . .
(*wincing as she plucks*)
if anyone can make you a star, Andy can.

VALERIE
Great—I'll go with you.

CANDY
(*clearly horrified at this prospect*)
Valerie, the invitation was to me *alone*.

VALERIE
I won't get in your way. I gotta meet him. I want to
show him my play.

EXTERIOR/INTERIOR: VALERIE'S ROOM, HOTEL EARLE. DAY.

Through the hotel window, we see VALERIE at a desk, banging at
an ancient typewriter.

VALERIE
(*voice-over*)
I dedicate this play to ME, a continuous source of
strength and guidance, and without whose unflinch-
ing loyalty, devotion, and faith this play would never
have been written.

Inside the room, the bed is unmade. There is a pile of typed pages on the desk beside VALERIE, and on top of that a handwritten page with the titles FROM THE CRADLE TO THE BOAT, THE BIG SUCK, and UP FROM THE SLIME crossed out, and the title UP YOUR ASS typed at the bottom. VALERIE carefully takes two pieces of blank paper, places a sheet of carbon paper between them, and inserts them in the typewriter.

> VALERIE
> (*voice-over*)
> Additional acknowledgments: Myself—for proof-reading, editorial comment, helpful hints, criticism and suggestions, and an exquisite job of typing. I— for independent research into men, married women, and other degenerates.

EXTERIOR: STREET NEAR THE FACTORY. DAY.

Breathless and teetering slightly on her spike heels, CANDY arrives at the doorway of a warehouse building, where VALERIE is waiting. VALERIE clutches a package in her arms.

> CANDY
> What's that?

VALERIE shows her the script. It has a red cover and the title printed in thick black letters.

> VALERIE
> It's my script. "Up Your Ass."

> CANDY
> Valerie, this is my big chance. Please don't embar-rass me. This is my chance to shine.

INTERIOR: THE FACTORY. DAY.

Darkness. The elevator doors open to reveal a vast expanse of silver, with figures moving hazily in the distance.

CANDY and VALERIE are standing in the entrance to the Factory, an enormous, shabby L-shaped loft painted silver, with Warhol silk screens stacked against the wall. Standing fans whir lazily. A huge, red broken-down couch is set against one wall.

They stand bewildered for a moment. Then CANDY gives VALERIE a warning look and walks down the length of the Factory, like Marlene Dietrich disappearing into the desert in *Morocco*, leaving VALERIE alone.

The following scene shows a series of quick, little vignettes, tableaux almost, as the camera follows VALERIE around the Factory. These scenes are shot in color but with a scheme that suggests black and white: silver walls, black clothes, white faces.

These Factory tableaux should be almost dreamlike: smoky, silver, glamorous, compared with the flatness and sordidness of Valerie's scenes. The Factory is an enclosed world, a haven from normality, where outside rules and regulations don't apply.

In the background, Maria Callas singing an aria from *Medea* blasts from the Factory record player.

The first thing VALERIE sees is:

SUSAN, a young, blond girl, in a corner, sitting lotus position at a low, silver desk with the legs sawn off. One of the legs is broken and is supported by a stack of magazines. She is typing transcripts from Warhol movies. We hear fragments of dialogue as the tape whizzes back and forth, and we hear the slow rhythmic sound of her typing, one key at a time.

VALERIE continues walking around the perimeter of the Factory, in and out of the shadows. She sees:

A young man painting something silver in a dark corner of the Factory, while another is carefully wrapping silver foil around steam pipes.

Close-up on their hands doing finicky, obsessive, drug-fueled work.

In the background, MORRISSEY is answering the phone. As he talks, he inspects his face in a piece of broken mirror glued next to the phone. Everyone who talks on the Factory phone does this.

> MORRISSEY
> Factory, hello? . . . Where the fuck have you been? Drella told me they delivered a camera, and there was no one here to receive it.

His conversation is heard in voice-over as the camera moves on.

> MORRISSEY
> (*voice-over*)
> Oh, you're having a *nervous breakdown?* What a re-lief. What a refreshing change . . .

Across the room, a partially open door beckons, glowing with an eerie red light. VALERIE wanders over and cautiously peers inside. It is a photographer's darkroom. BILLY NAME has his back to VALERIE as he bends over a sink.

VALERIE peers at him, half hidden by the open door.

Unaware that he is being watched, BILLY sings along with Maria Callas in the glow of the red light, as he swirls photographs in developing fluid. Other pictures are hanging up to dry: all the pictures are of Factory personnel. Some faces are recognizable, like Paul Morrissey and Susan. Others are faces we will meet later: Ondine, Viva, Brigid.

Moving through the shadows, VALERIE nearly stumbles over a pretty boy with curly hair, who is raptly drawing with Magic Markers in a trip book. He ignores her.

Rounding a corner, VALERIE sees two art assistants, GERARD, who is dark, and DANNY, who is blond, rolling silk screens of poppies, the only brilliant color in this scene.

Close-up of the rollers slowly moving back and forth, spreading color over the image.

ONDINE—a sardonic, gay speed freak—lolls on the big, red couch, ogling DANNY.

> ONDINE
> Listen, Danny, why don't you get those fucking girls
> from around your knees. The streets are just full of
> eligible men. Don't you want to become a woman?

> DANNY
> No!

> ONDINE
> No?!

> DANNY
> Not really.

> ONDINE
> Well, then, you'll never know what it is to be all
> woman, will you?

> GERARD
> You mean A.W.? Like Andy Warhol
> *(He chuckles to himself.)*
> A.W. can mean a lot of things. All woman. All witch.

> ONDINE
> *(ignoring him, addressing DANNY)*
> You mean you're going to spend all your life a . . .
> *bore?* Hovering between womanhood and manhood?
> No, be all woman and therefore all man. The first
> thing you have to do is to eat an asshole. I'll tell you
> how . . .

DANNY moves back without looking and knocks over a can of fuchsia-colored paint.

Close-up of the color slowly spreading over the floor. Hands trying to mop it up, getting stained with the vivid pink dye.

> DANNY
> Oh, shit. Andy's gonna kill me.

> GERARD
> Don't worry. He took his mother to church. He
> won't be back for hours.

Moving away, VALERIE sees VIVA talking on the silver pay phone
near the entrance. As VIVA talks, she watches herself in the mirror.
The following monologue runs underneath the action and is heard
only in fragments:

> VIVA
> Yeah, and my velvet dress is ruined. After all the hours
> I spent on airplanes sewing that lining. Someone
> dropped a lighted match on it, and I didn't notice
> until it was all burned up. I was so tired, and I took
> two Midols and a muscle relaxer and drank some
> wine that I made myself last Easter. Then I had two
> puffs on a pot cigarette, and I was so high I didn't
> notice . . . it was my favorite. The only other dress I
> like is a 1920s dress Andy bought, but it smells so
> of perspiration I can't wear it. Oh, who cares.

VALERIE has completed the circuit. She stands in the entranceway,
staring down the length of the Factory as the inhabitants come
and go, dreamily pursuing their various activities.
She looks up to see CANDY beside her.

> CANDY
> (*devastated*)

He's not here.

VALERIE
I know.

EXTERIOR: MIDTOWN STREET CORNER. DAY.

VALERIE paces back and forth, panhandling from passersby. Several passersby brush her off.

Walking along the street, she accosts MAURICE GIRODIAS, a distinguished-looking Frenchman in his late forties.

VALERIE
Could I interest you in some dirty words? I have a corner on the market.

GIRODIAS
(*confused*)
Excuse me?

VALERIE
Give me fifteen cents, and I'll give you a dirty word.

Still walking, GIRODIAS sighs wearily and digs into his pocket.

GIRODIAS
What's the word?

VALERIE
Men.

VALERIE pockets the change, still hurrying after him.

GIRODIAS
(*irritated*)
Why pick on me? Do I look like a tourist?

VALERIE
(*hurrying along beside him*)
No, you look like a connoisseur of conversation.
Want to buy an hour's worth for six bucks?

GIRODIAS
An hour's worth of *what?*

VALERIE
Conversation.

GIRODIAS
(*stopping in his tracks*)
You have a very original approach to earning a living.

VALERIE
How about it?

GIRODIAS
I'm very busy . . .

VALERIE
(*deadpan*)
Six dollars. One hour. Any subject you want.

GIRODIAS
A dollar for fifteen minutes.

VALERIE
Three dollars for thirty.

GIRODIAS
(*giving in*)
Oh, very well.
(*He adopts a courtly pose.*)

Would you care to have a glass of wine with me, and
a stimulating conversation?

>   VALERIE
>   (*sarcastic*)
> Enchanted, I'm sure. As long as you're paying.

INTERIOR: EL QUIXOTE BAR. AFTERNOON.

VALERIE and GIRODIAS are sitting in a booth. He is being charming
and courteous, pouring her wine. She is obviously pleased by the
attention.

GIRODIAS is amused by Valerie. At no point, either now or later,
does he show any real fear of her. Unlike Warhol, fear is not part
of Girodias's makeup: he believes himself to be invulnerable.

>   VALERIE
> So what do you wanna talk about?

>   GIRODIAS
> Let's talk about you. What do you do all day?

>   VALERIE
> Walk around the block a few times. Shoot the shit.
> Turn a few tricks . . .

>   GIRODIAS
> Tricks?

>   VALERIE
> You know: johns . . . sex . . . money? Sex for money.

>   GIRODIAS
> Oh ⸴ . . . are you happy doing that?

>   VALERIE
> Well, I meet a lot of fascinating people.

(She leans forward, conspiratorial.)
Like, the other day, I was standing on my usual corner, sneaking a free skim through the magazines,
when this old guy comes up to me . . .

As VALERIE says this, the light, sixties panhandling theme music
starts up.

EXTERIOR: GREENWICH VILLAGE NEWSSTAND. DAY.

VALERIE is standing at a magazine stand, scanning an article, "How
to Meet Men."
A repulsive OLD MAN comes up to her.

> VALERIE
> *(voice-over)*
> He said he didn't usually approach girls on the street,
> but I had a sympathetic face. Then he asked me a
> question . . .

VALERIE and the OLD MAN in conversation.

> OLD MAN
> Tell me—what do you do when you see a bug?

> VALERIE
> Step on it.

> OLD MAN
> Do you *like* to step on bugs?

> VALERIE
> Gets my rocks off every time.

> OLD MAN
> *(intense)*
> *Do* you? Do you like to hear them *crunch*?

VALERIE

Yeeaah!

OLD MAN

I *like* you. Yes, I like you *very* much. Do you always
wear tennis shoes?

VALERIE

Not when I'm in bed.

OLD MAN

Do you ever wear spiked heels? Or cowboy boots?
Or maybe even—

INTERIOR: EL QUIXOTE BAR. DAY.

VALERIE is leaning across the table, telling her story to GIRODIAS,
who is enthralled.

VALERIE

Now what could he be getting at? Oh no, I thought,
it's too much to hope for . . .

EXTERIOR: GREENWICH VILLAGE NEWSSTAND.
DAY.

OLD MAN
(*continuing*)
Do you like to wear *golf* shoes?

VALERIE

Only in bed.

OLD MAN
You know, you do have a flair for living.

The OLD MAN bares a chest pitted with scabs.

VALERIE
Golf shoes, I presume.

OLD MAN
Only this one.
(*He points to his chest.*)
The others are stiletto heels.

VALERIE
An exquisite mosaic.

Voice-over continues as we pull away from VALERIE and the OLD MAN talking in the street.

VALERIE
(*voice-over*)
He said he wanted to make it with me—once he'd bought me the proper shoes, of course.

INTERIOR: EL QUIXOTE BAR. DAY.

VALERIE
(*working her way through all the bowls of peanuts at the bar*)
I must have a real talent for chest stepping—he gave me twenty bucks. After that, knock off for a couple of days and write. I'm really a writer. I'm working on a play at the moment, based on some of my more enthralling encounters with the male species. It's called "Up Your Ass."

GIRODIAS
(*thoughtfully*)
"Up Your Ass" . . . so you're a writer? How interesting. I am a publisher.

VALERIE looks at him incredulously.

GIRODIAS
No, really. We have much more in common than you
think. You turn tricks for money; I sell dirty books.
Like you, I am not ashamed. But I also publish great
works of art. I own the Olympia Press—I've published many famous writers, and my books are known
all over the world: *Naked Lunch, Lolita, Candy* . . .
here, take my card.

VALERIE takes it and reads it suspiciously.

GIRODIAS
It's quite legitimate. You're wasting your talents on
the street, Valerie. You should write a novel. You
should write a novel for me.

VALERIE
Can I make money out of this?

GIRODIAS
Of course. I pay as much as two thousand dollars for
an advance.
(*He rummages through his briefcase and
pulls out a book.*)
Here, take one of our books. Compliments of Olympia Press, New York operation.

Close on the book as he hands it to her: a copy of Terry Southern's
Candy.

GIRODIAS

Maybe you'll write a best-seller—then you'll never have to work again.

(*As he checks his watch and hands her three dollars:*)

I'm quite serious. I'm interested in you. After all, I specialize in the subversive.

(*He gets up and gives her a little bow of farewell.*)

You can always reach me next door at the Chelsea Hotel.

VALERIE opens the book and looks at the frontispiece. As she reads, GIRODIAS is heard in voice-over:

GIRODIAS
(*voice-over*)

Notice to unknown writers: You have been rejected by all existing publishers: well and good, you have a chance with us. We read everything—promptly, discriminately, and optimistically. Send your manuscripts to Maurice Girodias, the Olympia Press . . .

INTERIOR: HOTEL EARLE LOBBY. DAY.

In the foreground, we see the Hotel Earle's television lounge. This is a room facing the street, with filthy blinds and battered furniture. A few guests sit watching an episode of *Dark Shadows* on an ancient television set. The guests are straight out of a Diane Arbus photograph: a catatonic Korean War veteran, an old lady and her daughter, a spinsterish woman in a flowered hat and rubber flip-flops.

In the background, we see VALERIE in the phone booth, dialing a number.

VALERIE

Hello, can I speak to Maurice Girodias, please . . . hello, it's Valerie

(*silence*)
. . . Valerie, you paid for my conversation, remember?

INTERIOR: OLYMPIA PRESS OFFICES. DAY.

The first part of this conversation is heard over a shot of a frosted-glass door with the words OLYMPIA PRESS freshly painted. During the following conversation, the camera travels around the room.

> GIRODIAS
> (*offscreen*)
> I remember, of course. What can I do for you?

Inside the office, which is littered with packing cases. During the telephone conversation, the camera moves around the room. It is very untidy, and the desk space and much of the floor are covered with stacks of books. These range from *Lolita*, Genet, and de Sade to piles of thin paperbacks with titles like *Curtain of Flesh* and *The Whipping Club*. On the cluttered desk are a half-empty bottle of red wine and a box of cigarettes.

> VALERIE
> (*offscreen*)
> Remember that play I was telling you about? Well,
> I'm having a read-through at Nedick's.

> GIRODIAS
> (*utterly confused*)
> Nedick's?

> VALERIE
> (*offscreen*)
> It's a restaurant. This reading—it's just an informal
> thing with some of my friends. They're mostly trans-
> vestites.

GIRODIAS
Of course.

VALERIE
(*offscreen*)
So do you wanna come?

GIRODIAS
The theater is not my specialty, I'm afraid. But please
let me know if you decide to write a novel. *That* I can
help you with. It's good to hear from you, Valerie. I
have to say good-bye to you now—good-bye.

INTERIOR: HOTEL EARLE LOBBY. DAY.
VALERIE sits in the phone booth, disconsolate, staring at the wall.
She picks up the phone and dials.

INTERIOR: THE FACTORY. DAY.
We see the phone on the wall ringing. The phone rings for a long
time unanswered.
In the middle distance, GERARD is carefully wrapping silk screens
in plastic and inserting them in cardboard boxes. WARHOL stops
by and remonstrates with him, showing a different way they should
be packed.
In one corner, MORRISSEY is supervising a screen test of BRIGID from
behind the camera.
In the background, a television crew have arrived, led by LAURA,
a pretty young reporter from the Canadian Broadcasting Corporation. We see WARHOL approach, with his back to us, and LAURA,
WARHOL, and GERARD chat as the camera circles round them.
In the foreground, SUSAN runs over and picks up the phone.

SUSAN
Hello, Factory? . . . I'm sorry, Andy's not here right
now.

(*She glances across the room at* WARHOL.)
Can you tell me what it's about? . . . Uh-huh . . . well,
you know Andy doesn't do theater . . . oh, I see. Uh-
huh . . . yes, I m sure it would make a very interesting movie. What's it called? Ooh . . .

SUSAN grimaces as she hears the title. By now she is convinced she
has a madwoman on the line but remains polite.

INTERIOR: HOTEL EARLE PHONE BOOTH. DAY.

VALERIE

Well, it' s "Up Your Ass" for now, but I have different titles. It's about how sleazy and disgusting men
are. It's a comedy. At the end, a mother kills her son.

VALERIE looks up at the sound of banging. The legless CONCIERGE
is banging on the glass of the phone booth.

VALERIE
(*opening the door and screaming*)
Fuck off!

The CONCIERGE bangs on the door again.

CONCIERGE
Get off the goddamn phone. Where's your rent, you
whore?

VALERIE pulls the door closed, hanging on to it with one hand
while she holds the phone in the other.

SUSAN
(*offscreen*)
Why don't you just drop it in the mail?

VALERIE

That's okay, I can bring it over right now.

INTERIOR: THE FACTORY. DAY.

The television interview is in progress.

LAURA

Why are you spending so much of your time on these
underground films?

WARHOL

They're uh . . . easier than making paintings.

LAURA

Do you think painting is dead?

WARHOL

Uh . . . no.

LAURA

But do you think that the cinema has more relevance?

WARHOL

Uh . . . no.

LAURA

Well, which of the modern painters do you find the
most significant?

WARHOL

Oh, I like all of them.

Cut to SUSAN at her desk. We see the interview carry on in the distance. SUSAN looks up from her typing and sees someone stepping out of the elevator. It is VALERIE.
SUSAN runs to the open door to head her off.

                    SUSAN
          Are you VALERIE?

                    VALERIE
          Yeah. I'm the writer.

                    SUSAN
              (*firmly blocking her path*)
          There's a TV interview going on right now.

                    VALERIE
          Can I watch?

                    SUSAN
          I'm sorry, no visitors today. Just leave me the script;
          I'll make sure Andy gets it.

VALERIE clutches the script as if she can't bear to part with it.

                    VALERIE
              (*fretful*)
          I really wanted to give it to him in person.

SUSAN smiles politely and shakes her head, continuing to block Valerie's path.

                    VALERIE
              (*holding it out to* SUSAN)
          Okay. But look after it. I only have one other copy.

Reluctantly, VALERIE hands the script over. It has a bright red cover with UP YOUR ASS written in thick, black Magic Marker.

INTERIOR: NEDICK'S. DAY.

The drag queens are gathered by the kitchen at the back of the restaurant to watch a rehearsal of Valerie's play. Every so often, the doors fly open, and a busboy or waitress rushes past, carrying a tray and cursing them for getting in the way.

In the background, the restaurant carries on as usual, with its familiar collection of outcasts bent over their hot dogs.

> STEVIE
> *(holding a script in her hand as she reads*
> *the stage directions)*
> Up Your Ass by Valerie Solanas. Time: The present; afternoon. Place: A large American city; the sidewalk. Bongi Perez is loitering on the steps of an apartment building where she lives.

VALERIE, playing Bongi, saunters across the room.

> STEVIE
> A broad passes by.

A drag queen walks in front of her, swinging her hips.

> VALERIE
> *(as Bongi)*
> *Hello*, beautiful.

The "broad" ignores her.

> VALERIE
> *(as Bongi)*

Stuck-up bitch.
> (*Calling after the broad:*)

Oh my, but aren't we the high-class ass. You got a
twat by Dior?

Enter CANDY as Ginger, a girl in her middle twenties dressed like
a Barbie doll. CANDY makes her entrance from the ladies' room.
She teeters over to VALERIE on her high heels and sneaks a look at
the script. From now on, they share the script, sometimes reading the lines, sometimes saying them from memory.

>   CANDY
>   (*as Ginger*)
> Say, miss, did you, by any chance, see a turd any-
> where around here?

>   VALERIE
>   (*as Bongi*)
> What's it look like? Is it blue?

>   CANDY
>   (*as Ginger*)
> No, no, no, no.

>   VALERIE
>   (*as Bongi*)
> Is it green?

>   CANDY
>   (*as Ginger*)
> *No*, no, no, no.

>   VALERIE
>   (*as Bongi*)
> Is it red?

CANDY
(*as Ginger*)
NO! NO! NOO! NO! Just a little, yellow turdlet.

VALERIE
(*as Bongi*)
Not to be nosy, but does this turd have sentimental value?

CANDY
(*as Ginger*)
Don't be absurd. It's for dinner.

VALERIE
(*as Bongi*)
Oh. Why would it be rolling around out here?

Forgetting her lines, CANDY teeters over to STEVIE to get a quick peek at the script.

CANDY
(*as Ginger*)
I took it out to have it dyed yellow, and it must have dropped out of the bag when I was coming in.

VALERIE
(*as Bongi*)
Do you often have turd for dinner?

INTERIOR: THE FACTORY. DAY.
Several Warholites—BRIGID, VIVA, SUSAN—are sitting on the red couch, sharing a single script, reading the play aloud to WARHOL. The reading carries on exactly where the previous extract left off.

> VIVA
> (*as Ginger*)
> You're really too much. Would you want to be eating turds all the time?

> VIVA
> (*looking up*)
> Can you believe this? This is so *sick*!

They carry on with the reading.

INTERIOR: NEDICK'S. DAY.

VALERIE and CANDY in their roles.

> VALERIE
> (*as Bongi*)
> You do have a point there.

> CANDY
> (*as Ginger*)
> I'm having company tonight. I'm having two really dynamic, fascinating men over for dinner, and I want to make the best possible impression.

> VALERIE
> (*as Bongi*)
> So you're serving them a turd.

> CANDY
> (*as Ginger*)
> You're im*pos*sible. I assure you, I have no intention whatsoever of serving my guests a turd. The turd's for me. Everybody knows that men have much more

respect for women who're good at lapping up shit.
Say, would you like to join us for dinner?

INTERIOR: THE FACTORY. DAY.

The Warholites look at each other.

> BRIGID
> This is too revolting, even for us.

BRIGID tosses the manuscript behind the couch. The conversation
turns to another topic.

INTERIOR: NEDICK'S. DAY.

VALERIE and CANDY are still "onstage."
Offscreen, a voice is heard yelling "Cut!"
It comes from the MANAGER, who is standing on the sidelines.

> MANAGER
> You're in a restaurant, not on Broadway. Order
> something or get out. And stop blocking the exits.

EXTERIOR: HOTEL EARLE. DAY.

VALERIE hovers just outside the door. She peers through the glass,
starts to open the door, then quickly backs away, skulking in the
doorway. She repeats the process. After peering through the glass
again, she opens the door and makes a run inside.

INTERIOR: HOTEL EARLE. DAY.

VALERIE is running up the stairs, pursued by a policeman, as the
CONCIERGE screams after her:

CONCIERGE
Give me your rent, you whore!

EXTERIOR: ROOFTOP. DAWN.

The sound of typing floats over shots of the city at dawn. VALERIE
is huddled on the same rooftop that we saw her on when she first
arrived in New York. Her possessions—two shopping bags, a typewriter case—are gathered around her. A sheaf of notes written
on torn-up brown paper bags lies beside her. The typewriter is
on her knees, and she is typing furiously: a document headed
SOCIETY FOR CUTTING UP MEN: THE SCUM MANIFESTO.

VALERIE
(*voice-over*)
Presentation of the rationale and program of action
of SCUM, Society for Cutting up Men . . .

EXTERIOR: WEST SIDE PIER. DUSK.

Dusk coming down on an empty street leading down to the river.
The water.
An abandoned warehouse. From a distance, we see VALERIE and a
JOHN leaning up against the side of one wall.
Cut to close-up: from now on, we only see her head and shoul-
ders, with the back of the man's head occasionally moving into
frame.
Valerie's face looks blank as her head is jerked back and forth,
banging against the wall.

VALERIE
(*voice-over*)
Unhampered by propriety, "niceness," discretion,
public opinion, "morals," the "respect" of assholes,
always funky, dirty, low down . . .

EXTERIOR: ROOFTOP. DAY.

VALERIE is still huddled in a corner, banging away on the type-writer. A little pile of cigarette butts indicates the passage of time.

> VALERIE
> (*voice-over*)
> SCUM gets around . . . and around and around . . .
> they've covered the whole waterfront—

EXTERIOR: WEST SIDE PIER. DUSK.

The sound of typing merges into the sound of Valerie's head banging against the wall.

> VALERIE
> (*voice-over continuing*)
> Been under every dock and pier—the peter pier, the
> pussy pier. You've got to go through a lot of sex to
> get to antisex, and SCUM's been through it all . . .

EXTERIOR: ROOFTOP. DAY.

VALERIE is typing.

> VALERIE
> (*voice-over continuing*)
> And now they're ready for a new show; they want
> to crawl out from under the dock, move, take off,
> sink out . . .

EXTERIOR: WEST SIDE PIER. DAY.

Close-up of VALERIE, the back of the man's head obscuring her face as he groans and collapses against her as he comes.
His head withdraws from the frame.

A hand reaches into the frame and ruffles her hair mockingly.
Close-up of her face—blank, hostile—staring back.
A hand shoves a wad of dollar bills into her mouth.

INTERIOR: CHELSEA HOTEL. DAY.

The reception desk.
Close-up of Valerie's hands counting out a wad of crumpled dollar
bills and passing them under the grille.

> VALERIE
>
> Twenty-two . . . twenty-three . . . twenty-four . . .
> twenty-five.

> MANAGER
>
> It would be cheaper if you paid by the month.

VALERIE shakes her head.

> VALERIE
>
> Can you put me through to Maurice Girodias's
> room?

> MANAGER
>
> Monsieur Girodias has gone away for a few days.

> VALERIE
>
> (*disappointed, annoyed*)
> Well, can I get a bellboy to help with this stuff?

The MANAGER gives her a look, as if to say, "You must be kidding."

INTERIOR: VALERIE'S ROOM, CHELSEA HOTEL. DAY.

VALERIE is sitting on her bed, dialing a number on the telephone.

VALERIE

Hi, this is Valerie Solanas. I'm calling again about
the script I left with you . . . well, can I talk to Andy?
Oh, okay . . . I'll call back.

VALERIE hangs up. A long pause, and then she picks up the phone
and dials again.

VALERIE
(*adopting a breathy, affected voice*)
Hello, this is Candy Darling. I want to make an ap-
pointment with Andy Warhol for later this evening.
Will he be there? Oh, good.

INTERIOR: THE FACTORY. NIGHT.

Close-up of changing textures of walls and grates. We hear the
sinister elevator theme music that we will hear later in the film
but played very lyrically and innocuously. This is the old Factory
elevator, an open cage. VALERIE steps right out into the silver Factory.
WARHOL stands with GERARD in a pool of light halfway down the
room, lit by a hanging electric bulb. There are photographs spread
out on a table in front of him, strips from a photo booth, showing a smiling blond woman.
VALERIE walks very slowly toward them. At first they don't notice
her.

VALERIE

Andy Warhol?

WARHOL looks up, his face catching the light. This is the first time
we see his face. He looks surprisingly young and vulnerable.

VALERIE

I'm Valerie Solanas.

WARHOL looks blank.

> VALERIE
> I sent you my play. "Up Your Ass."

> WARHOL
> Oh yeah. It's such a great title. But it's so dirty!

> GERARD
> Yeah—it was *so* dirty we thought it must be some kind of entrapment.

> WARHOL
> We thought you were a lady cop.

> VALERIE
> (*unzipping her jeans and exposing herself*)
> Sure I am, and here's my badge.

The two men stare at her, nonplussed.

> WARHOL
> Do you want to do a screen test?

INTERIOR: THE FACTORY. A FEW NIGHTS LATER.

Flashing black-and-white film leader.

Pull out to reveal a sheet hanging at one end of the Factory on which black-and-white film portraits—static shots of various members of the Factory—are projected. Each one is introduced by film leader and flashes. Sometimes we see the portraits full screen; at others, we see Factory life going on behind and around the screen. Present in the Factory are VIVA, IRIS, BILLY, GERARD, BRIGID, JACKIE, CURTIS, and ONDINE. We will see film portraits of Morrissey, Gerard, Brigid, Ultra Violet, Viva, Valerie, and superstar.

MORRISSEY is standing by the projector, talking to LAURA. Her cameraman and sound recordist are lurking in the background, fiddling with their equipment.

> MORRISSEY
> I want to move out of here, so we can really get organized, get rid of some of the craziness, move full-time into producing films. These are some of our screen tests . . .
> *(he examines a piece of film as he feeds it into the projector)*
> We have so many fabulous personalities here—the Factory is a lot like the old MGM star system.

> LAURA
> Are you serious?

> MORRISSEY
> Oh sure. We believe in stars, and our kids are actually very similar to the Walt Disney kids, except of course that they're *modern* children, so naturally they take drugs and have sex.

Cut to a group of Factory habitués, who lounge around watching the screening, lying on cushions, smoking joints. Sitting on the sofa at the back are JACKIE and ONDINE, who provide a running commentary on each film.

The first screen test is GERARD, who is looking at himself very intently in the mirror, combing his hair.

> JACKIE
> *(offscreen)*
> Look, it's Adonis.

ONDINE
(*offscreen*)
Oh, Mary, can you believe her?

JACKIE
Who does she think she is: "Look at me, I'm
straight."

ONDINE
Yeah, straight for my dick.

Cut to flickering black-and-white film leader, followed by a portrait of BRIGID lounging back in a chair. She stares straight into
the camera then, without shifting her gaze, brings out a syringe
and jabs it into her butt. She injects herself right through her jeans.

ONDINE
(*offscreen*)
Oh, my God, the Duchess. Desperate for attention,
as usual.

JACKIE
(*offscreen*)
She's an evil pig, but Andy likes to have her around.
I don't know why.

Next, a series of portraits: three beautiful female superstars.
In the first portrait, ULTRA VIOLET sits on the sofa, applying makeup,
using her compact mirror.

ONDINE
(*voice-over*)
Beat that face, bitch.

Next portrait: Superstar Number One.

JACKIE
(*voice-over*)
I hear Joe gave her crabs.

Next portrait: Superstar Number Two.

ONDINE
(*voice-over*)
Now *she* is lovely. She has that fragile, nervous-breakdown quality.

JACKIE
(*voice-over*)
Think Andy'll keep her around?

ONDINE
(*voice-over*)
Maybe. Her family came over on the Mayflower.

Next portrait: MORRISSEY with a camera, shooting himself in the mirror.

ONDINE
Cecil B. de Mille
(*pause*)
Junior.

JACKIE
We've got to get rid of him. He's power mad.

Next, Candy Darling's portrait: CANDY flirting with the camera.

ONDINE
(*offscreen*)
Oooh, she's beautiful.

JACKIE
(*offscreen*)

That's my friend Candy.

ONDINE
(*offscreen*)

She is *so* real.

JACKIE

She's realer than real.

Finally, a portrait of VALERIE looking lost and uneasy in front of the camera.

JACKIE
(*offscreen*)

Ugh, what's that?

ONDINE

Isn't she tragic?

JACKIE

Look at her hair. So mannish.

ONDINE

She's a manhater. What does Andy see in her?

JACKIE

Maybe he feels sorry for her. She won't last.

ONDINE

Honey, she scares me.

The camera follows DANNY as he walks to the opposite end of the Factory, bringing some equipment to WARHOL, who is painting in areas of a silk screen.

VALERIE sits on her heels watching WARHOL, who is totally absorbed
in his work.

> VALERIE
>
> So, Andy, I really wanna get my play produced. Have
> you read it yet?

> WARHOL
>
> Oh, Valerie, I'm sure it's fabulous.

> VALERIE
>
> You should produce it. With your flair for public-
> ity, it could make a fortune. We could start on off
> Broadway.

> ANDY
> (*not paying attention*)
> Oh, that sounds great.

> VALERIE
>
> I need some more actors. All I have is drag queens.
> Maybe I'll put an ad in one of the underground rags.

INTERIOR: NEDICK'S. DAY.

Close-up of an underground newspaper, the *East Village Other*,
held up by CANDY, who is reading the want ads aloud.
CANDY and JACKIE CURTIS are sitting in a booth with their friend
JEREMIAH. He is a tall, good-looking boy, about eighteen, with
long, brown hair and a sweet, rather naive manner.

> CANDY
>
> "Wanted: Hip girl typist—part-time, East Village
> area. Groovy, unbusinesslike atmosphere." That
> sounds fun.

JACKIE

You can't type, honey. How about this? "Wanted—
A young, shapely girl who wants to supplement her
income easily by dating affluent but busy bachelor
occasionally in his apartment.
Teenybopper OK. Write: PO Box 56, NYC 1125."

CANDY
(*thinks for a moment*)
I'm not a teenybopper.

CANDY keeps leafing through the classifieds, searching for something.

CANDY

I want to find the ad for Valerie's play.
(*proudly*)
I'm playing the ingenue . . . here it is . . .
(*She reads aloud:*)
"SCUM, Society for Cutting up Men, is looking for
garbage-mouth dykes, butch or fem, with some acting ability, experience not necessary to appear in
garbage-mouth dykey antimale play, a comedy, called
'Up Your Ass.'"

JACKIE

Valerie? Is that the dyke who lives down the hall from
you?

CANDY

She did, but they kicked her out. She couldn't pay
her rent, so she moved somewhere more expensive.
The Chelsea. It's very artistic.
(*She continues reading aloud.*)

"Also looking for talented garbage-mouth, pretty, effeminate-looking males"—
(*they look at* JEREMIAH *meaningfully*)
—"and regular, straight-looking males. If interested in trying out for a role, call the Chelsea Hotel."

JACKIE
She's *nuts*.

CANDY
Valerie's okay. She s a little funny about men. But she'll like you, Jeremiah; you should call her.

INTERIOR: VALERIE'S ROOM, CHELSEA HOTEL. DAY.
VALERIE sits smoking on the bed in her hotel room, talking on the phone.

VALERIE
HELLO? I'M HAVING TROUBLE WITH MY PHONE—CAN YOU HEAR ME?

JEREMIAH
(*offscreen*)
Yes, I can hear you. It's about the audition.

VALERIE
Meet me in the lobby of the Chelsea Hotel tonight at 9 P.M., and I'll read you. What's your name?

JEREMIAH
(*offscreen*)
Jeremiah.

VALERIE

What do you look like?

JEREMIAH
(*offscreen*)
Tall with long, brown hair. What do you look like?

VALERIE

A butch dyke.

VALERIE hangs up.

INTERIOR: CHELSEA HOTEL LOBBY. DAY.

JEREMIAH stands waiting in the Chelsea Hotel lobby. VALERIE stalks in, muttering something insulting to the MANAGER as she passes. The BELL CLERK glares at her. She is wearing a man's cap; a brown, imitation-suede coat; faded sweatshirt; and jeans. She stares at JEREMIAH and calls him over. Then she asks for the key to the basement.

VALERIE
(*unlocking the basement door*)
Just don't touch the steam pipes.

INTERIOR: CHELSEA HOTEL BASEMENT. DAY.

VALERIE
(*as she ushers* JEREMIAH *into the darkness*)
I'm not going to kill you. I just don't want to take you to my room because you'll damage my reputation.

They sit on a steep staircase, with trails of steam rising from below. The roar of a generator can be heard from the depths of the cellar. The stairs are lit by a single bare electric bulb. JEREMIAH sits uneasily near the top of the steps; VALERIE places herself a few steps below. She hands him a dog-eared script. VALERIE herself will read from memory:

VALERIE

Here. You read Russell.
(*She points to a place:*)
Start here.

JEREMIAH
(*as Russell, with an unconvincing attempt at macho aggression*)

No! The two-sex system *must* be right; it's survived hundreds of thousands of years.

VALERIE
(*as Bongi*)

So has disease.

JEREMIAH
(*as Russell*)

You can't just determine us away. We won't allow it; we'll unite; we'll fight.

VALERIE
(*as Bongi*)

You may as well resign yourself: eventually the expression "female of the species" will be a redundancy.

JEREMIAH
(*as Russell*)

You don't know what a female is, you de-sexed monstrosity.

> VALERIE
> (*as Bongi*)
> On the contrary, I'm so female I'm subversive.

INTERIOR: NEDICK'S. DAY.

VALERIE and JEREMIAH are talking over hot dogs at the counter. CANDY and friends are at a table behind them. Two Vietnam War veterans, one in a wheelchair, are at another table.

> VALERIE
> (*gesturing toward the veterans*)
> Look at this shitty war we're in—if a woman was in charge, it would never have happened.

> JEREMIAH
> (*sadly*)
> I'm expecting my draft papers any day now . . .

> VALERIE
> Women are real; they're human. Men aren't even complete human beings: the male gene is an incomplete female gene. That's why he's got this built-in inferiority complex and is always pulling all his lousy stunts.

VALERIE takes a vicious bite of her hot dog.

> JEREMIAH
> Do you want to kill all the men in the world?

VALERIE

No, not all men—I don't think that will be necessary. The male, thank God, is gradually eliminating
himself.

A shriek of laughter distracts VALERIE and JEREMIAH. CANDY, who is
sitting at an adjacent table, puts an entire hot dog in her mouth
suggestively, then pulls it out. Her companions applaud approvingly.

JEREMIAH
(*whispering discreetly*)
What about drag queens?

VALERIE
(*loudly and tactlessly*)
What about drag queens?

JEREMIAH
Well, I mean . . . they want to be women, so . . .

VALERIE

You mean, if you got a sex change, would you be
okay? *No.* You're still a man. It's not what makes a
woman a woman, *hormones.* There's more to it than
that. Look at Candy Darling—

CANDY perks up at hearing her name mentioned.

VALERIE
(*continuing*)
Here you have a perfect victim of male suppression.

CANDY
(*to her table*)
Piffle.

JEREMIAH
What about *gay* men—would they be hurt?

VALERIE
Nah, gay men are okay. As I say in my manifesto: "By their shimmering, flaming example, they encourage other men to de-man themselves." I have big plans for some gay men.

INTERIOR: THE FACTORY STAIRCASE. NIGHT.

VALERIE climbs the stairs to the Factory, a little out of breath. She stops and checks the nameplate on one of the doors: it is the headquarters of the American Communist Party. Music is playing in the distance. As she ascends the next flight of stairs, the music becomes louder.

As she opens the door a blast of deafening rock music hits her. Through the doorway, we see a smoky, crowded room.

INTERIOR: THE FACTORY. NIGHT.

Reverse angle: VALERIE in the doorway.

Behind her the elevator doors open to reveal a group of extremely glamorous Europeans, led by the COMTESSE DE COURCY and her young cousin ISABELLE DE COURCY, and LAURA, the Canadian reporter. The men are in dark suits and narrow ties; the women, in black cocktail dresses and chignons. They pour out of the elevator, and VALERIE is swept into the Factory along with them.

GERARD rushes forward to greet the Italians. VALERIE watches as he politely greets LAURA.

Ignoring VALERIE, GERARD shepherds the Italians across the room to meet WARHOL.

We follow Valerie's gaze as she looks down the Factory: a rock band is at one end, on a makeshift stage, tuning up for their next song. Young people drift past the canvasses stacked against the wall as if they were wandering through an art exhibition.

The following party scenes will overlap or run simultaneously, and much of the dialogue will be heard only in fragments.

The camera follows Valerie's point of view as she moves down the Factory, past a cluster of people standing or sitting on a stepladder, toward a group sitting on the floor, beneath a film that is being projected onto a sheet hanging on the wall. The film features VIVA and GERARD kissing.

As VALERIE moves in on the little group in front of the projection screen, she sees they are not interested in the images on the screen but in a huge pile of multicolored pills and capsules on the floor in front of them. BRIGID is sifting through a handful of the pills as a small group of amphetamine addicts watch her intently. They include a flamboyantly dressed boy named ROTTEN RITA.

Close-up of BRIGID's hands sifting through the pills.

> ROTTEN RITA
> What are those marvelous tabs called, the white ones
> with the blue speckles?

> BRIGID
> Those are called Adasap.

> ROTTEN RITA
> Ooh, is that methamphetamine hydrochloric?

> A-HEAD
> It's the same as the zoxin. It's a brand name.

The conversation drifts out over other party images.

> ROTTEN RITA
> (*voice-over*)
> I'm stuck with these twenty milligram bi-phetamines,
> but they make me feel funny. Do you have any
> Obetrol?

BRIGID

Orange ones. Ten milligrams.

ROTTEN RITA

Oh, the orange ones are divine . . .

Cut to a montage of early party activity: MORRISSEY and DANNY are standing by the projector. They are trying out a new strobe, bouncing light against a big, mirrored disco ball and onto the faces of the band.

MORRISSEY

You call this a groovy light show? I'd rather watch a clothes dryer in a Laundromat.

ONDINE places a tab of acid on Iris's tongue. She is on her knees with her hands folded, as if receiving the sacrament. A line of other supplicants waits behind her.

Cut to the entrance. A group of teenyboppers arrives, squealing, jumping up and down, and waving to GERARD to try and attract his attention. They snake through the party to jump up and down in front of the band.

Cut to the band on stage. MORRISSEY has sorted out the strobe. DANNY is spooling film through the projector, occasionally slipping a different colored gel onto the lens. There are images projected everywhere: against the stage backdrop, over the band, over the faces of the crowd; images over images, huge blown-up faces of the superstars covered in hypnotically swirling dot patterns.

WARHOL is operating the spotlight, which he has trained on GERARD onstage. GERARD is doing his S&M dance, twirling whips and flashlights, as his face is projected on the screen behind him.

Cut to ONDINE sitting at the very top of a huge stepladder, surveying the swirling party scene. VALERIE climbs up the ladder, ruthlessly stepping on the people seated at the bottom, who complain loudly.

ONDINE

The oracle is open.

VALERIE

What?

ONDINE

It's Saturday—the oracle is open. What do you want
to ask the oracle?

VALERIE

Nothing.

ONDINE

Then get out of Delphi. You have no right to come
up here and waste the oracle's time.

Ignoring him, VALERIE stares down at the crowd below. The room
is packed and smoky. The little group of teenyboppers are forc-
ing their way into the center, toward WARHOL, causing ripples of
movement in the crowd. VALERIE watches LAURA dancing on her
own in front of the band, her eyes on GERARD as he does his whip
dance.
Cut to the amphetamine heads.
Close-up of the pills spread out on the floor. Now we see what
BRIGID has been up to. She is arranging all the pills and capsules
in an elaborate pattern: a mandala. The A-heads stare at it greed-
ily. One leans over and tries to take a pill. BRIGID slaps his hand
away.

BRIGID

Don't mess it up!

Cut to VALERIE approaching LAURA.

                            VALERIE
Hi. My name's Valerie.

                            LAURA
Hi, I'm Laura.

                            VALERIE
Yeah, um, I'm the leader of a new revolutionary
organization. It's called SCUM—the Society for
Cutting up Men. I'd love you to be a member.

                            LAURA
                         (*impressed*)
You kill men?

                            VALERIE
Uh, no, not yet, not yet. You want to be a member?

                            LAURA
I can't be a member. You see, I'm a reporter; I have
to remain very neutral. But thank you.

GERARD jumps off the stage and heads toward LAURA.

                            VALERIE
Well, I'd love to do an interview.

                            LAURA
That'd be groovy actually . . . uh, could you send me
some literature?

GERARD grabs LAURA and leads her away.

                            VALERIE
                      (*calling after her*)
I got the manifesto right here—it's for free!

A squeal from the teenyboppers as GERARD jumps off the stage and makes his way through the crowd. The teenyboppers fall into each others arms in mock faints, calling out, "Adonis! Adonis!"
Later:
BRIGID has stripped to the waist. The other amphetamine-heads are in various stages of undress.

> ROTTEN RITA
> Dexies don't do anything at all. You know what I dig? I dig those round pink ones. Prelude.

> A-HEAD
> Prelude? I thought they were antipregnancy pills.

> ROTTEN RITA
> (*nauseated*)
> Oh, don't, are you kidding?

> BRIGID
> (*ferociously*)
> Stop taking them. I tell you, 'cause I really know the trip of the pill. I don't take uppies any more.

With a single gesture, BRIGID sweeps away the mandala pattern and scatters the pills all over the floor, as the amphetamine-heads gasp and grab at them.

> BRIGID
> (*calmly*)
> I just take my pokes. I'm finished with pills.

BRIGID takes out a syringe, pulls down her jeans, and jabs a needle into her butt.
Across the room, the COMTESSE DE COURCY notices what is going on, and her eyes widen as BRIGID injects herself.
The COMTESSE and ISABELLE DE COURCY are in conversation with FRED HUGHES. ONDINE walks out of a backroom, holding a large,

open jar of Vaseline in one hand; a naked boy is visible through the doorway. ONDINE greets FRED effusively, much to Fred's embarrassment.

> FRED
>
> Uh . . . this is Ondine . . . uh . . . one of the greatest . actors in underground film today.

> ONDINE
> (*charmingly*)
>
> Oh, I'm *so* glad you said that, because most people confuse me with being a vulgar pig.

Later:
The band is taking a break, and pop records blare through the amps.
VALERIE sits on the floor, looking up at the teenyboppers, who are shimmying to the music. Low angle shots of their white boots and vinyl miniskirts, fishnet tights, and little pocketbooks swinging as they dance in a line together.
GERARD and LAURA dance. VALERIE sits on the edge of the crowd watching them. WARHOL, who is standing by the light of the projector, is watching them too. VALERIE glances over at WARHOL. Their eyes meet.
Cut to ONDINE, FRED, the COMTESSE, and ISABELLE. ONDINE is in mid-monologue:

> ONDINE
>
> And that's what I hate about transvestites. If you can't do what you want without *any* clothes on— *least* of all women's—then you shouldn't have sex at all.

The COMTESSE and ISABELLE have a brief discussion in French about what he might be talking about.

ONDINE

And for the last time, what is a *gay* bar? What *is* it?
Can you tell me? . . .
(*Another brief flurry of perplexed French.*)
As a homosexual, I will not go to one—why should
I be segregated?

FRED
(*firmly pushing him away*)
That's right—you should be *isolated*.

Cut to IRIS in a corner, staring at her face in a hand mirror and
laughing.
Cut to CANDY and JACKIE sitting in another corner, whispering
together. They are very, very stoned. JACKIE is wearing mascara
but is otherwise dressed as a boy tonight, in a sailor cap and
stubble; CANDY is in full drag.
VALERIE comes up to them. They look up, their eyes blurry and
unfocused. CANDY acknowledges VALERIE with a wave of her hand
and a vague smile, and sinks back into the sofa. JACKIE turns to a
boy next to him, and they kiss. CANDY gives JACKIE a dirty look
and pretends to ignore them, looking in a small hand mirror and
applying lipstick in an exaggerated, sophisticated manner.
Later: VALERIE and WARHOL sit at opposite ends of the big, red
couch, in silence, watching the party. They look at each other.

WARHOL

Hi.

VALERIE

Hi.

WARHOL holds out his tape recorder.

WARHOL

Say something.

VALERIE looks up at him, bewildered.

> WARHOL
> I have a great idea. I thought maybe you could just
> do a whole monologue for an hour for me.

> VALERIE
> No, I don't wanna do that, really.

> WARHOL
> You can sing, or talk . . . anything.

> VALERIE
> No, I can't, honestly.
> (*Sarcastically:*)
> I can only talk for that long when I have a stimulat-
> ing person like yourself to talk to.

> WARHOL
> Oh, come on, Valerie. Say something dirty.

A moment of silence as VALERIE tries to think.

> WARHOL
> Sex is really nothing, isn't it?

> VALERIE
> (*suddenly inspired*)
> I'm gonna read you something I've written. It's from
> my latest masterpiece, the "SCUM Manifesto" . . .

VALERIE pulls out a worn notebook and riffles through it until she
finds what she is looking for. She leans toward the microphone
that WARHOL holds out to her.

VALERIE
Sex is the refuge of the mindless . . . sex is not part
of a relationship; on the contrary, it is a solitary experience, noncreative, a gross waste of time.

WARHOL
Oh, that's *great*, Valerie.

VALERIE
(*encouraged by his response*)
The female can easily—far more easily than she may
think—condition away her sex drive, leaving her
completely cool and cerebral and free to pursue truly
worthy relationships and activities . . .

Music. The band members are back onstage. The opening chords
of a song float under the last part of Valerie's speech: the Velvet
Underground's "I'm Set Free."
Cut to the band playing. The music continues over the following scenes:
The sofa from behind: back shot of VALERIE and ANDY deep in
conversation, very late-night party action in the background.
BRIGID rolls in the spilled amphetamines so colored pills and capsules stick all over her naked breasts and back.
Amphetamine-heads are running around with shopping bags filled
with multicolored glitter, throwing handfuls over everyone.
ONDINE swings a needle, having just given someone a shot, send-
ing an arc of blood spurting in a strobe flash and spattering across
a face in the crowd.

IRIS
(*hallucinating on acid, looking in the mirror
and crying*)
I'm so ugly, I'm so ugly, I'm so ugly.

EXTERIOR: FACTORY ROOF. NIGHT.

ROTTEN RITA, ONDINE, and BILLY NAME are chasing each other around, throwing handfuls of glitter. A couple of male sex scenes are also going on up on the roof but are barely discernible in the shadows.

Shots of the city at night: the all-night coffeeshop across the street; the empty newsstand; the building from the streets, little figures running around on top, the glow of lights from the Factory windows.

INTERIOR: THE FACTORY. NIGHT.

The darkroom: In the red light of the darkroom, a hand plunges into the water, disturbing the photos. It is Gerard's hand, searching for balance as he props himself against the sink. GERARD and LAURA are having sex in the backroom. Her legs are wrapped around his waist . . .

WARHOL is peeking at them through a crack in the door.

INTERIOR: THE FACTORY. DAWN.

ONDINE sits on a windowsill, smoking a cigarette, watching the sun come up.

EXTERIOR: STREETS. DAWN.

Shots of dawn coming up over the streets leading to the river.

INTERIOR: THE FACTORY. DAWN.

The breeze from the fans stirs the silver foil on the walls.

VALERIE is curled up, peacefully asleep on the sofa.

BILLY NAME is sweeping up the detritus, a litter of paper cups, cigarette butts, syringes—all of it covered in a fine dust of multi-colored glitter. As he passes VALERIE, he stops sweeping for a moment, picks up a jacket lying near the sofa, and gently places it over her. He carries on sweeping.

EXTERIOR: CHELSEA HOTEL. DAY.

A shot of the outside of the Chelsea Hotel, accompanied by the onscreen title SUMMER 1967 and by music from Love's *Forever Changes.*

INTERIOR: CHELSEA HOTEL LOBBY. DAY.

VALERIE sits bolt upright against a bench in the lobby, like a statue, staring intently at the people coming in and out. She is in her usual outfit of baggy man's shirt, jeans, sailor's cap. Her eyes flicker back and forth across the room; she is obviously waiting for someone. Cut to the reception area. In the foreground, GIRODIAS approaches the desk to collect his mail. Before he gets there, he is waylaid by the MANAGER.

VALERIE is in the background, still bolt upright against the wall.

> MANAGER
>
> I'm sorry, Monsieur Girodias, but . . . the rent.

> GIRODIAS
>
> Oh, my dear fellow, I'm so sorry. My distributor was supposed to deliver a check this morning. These damned people are so unreliable. You know how it is . . .

Cut to VALERIE, watching GIRODIAS from across the room. GIRODIAS is now collecting his mail.

He turns round and is startled to see VALERIE staring up at him.

> VALERIE
>
> Remember me?

For a moment, GIRODIAS looks absolutely blank.

> VALERIE
> I'm ready to write that novel.

There is a slowly dawning recognition in Girodias's face as VALERIE continues to stare up at him.

> GIRODIAS
> Of course . . .
> (*obviously struggling to think of what to do*)
> we must discuss this . . .
> (*writing something down*)
> call me next week, and we'll arrange to have dinner.
> I'll prepare a contract.

INTERIOR: MAX'S KANSAS CITY. NIGHT.

VALERIE is making her way from table to table, hawking the manifesto. Someone greets her.

> VALERIE
> Got any money? It's only a dollar.

VALERIE sees CANDY across the room. CANDY waves at her regally, acknowledging her but keeping her at a distance.
Cut to WARHOL and a small group of friends, observing VALERIE as she draws nearer to them.

> WARHOL
> There's Valerie Solanas. Why don't you talk to her, Viva?

VALERIE approaches WARHOL, VIVA, and BRIGID. VALERIE is very shy and hesitant in their company. She hands WARHOL a copy of the manifesto.

Andy Warhol (Jared Harris) on the Factory pay phone
© Joyce George, courtesy of Orion Pictures Corporation

Lili Taylor as Valerie Solanas
© Joyce George, courtesy of Orion Pictures Corporation

Jared Harris as Andy Warhol

Stevie (Martha Plimpton) and Valerie (Lili Taylor) in the Hotel Earle

Valerie accosts Warhol and his entourage at Max's Kansas City

Director Mary Harron with Lili Taylor on the Revolutionary's bedroom set

© Bill Foley, courtesy of Orion Pictures Corporation

Gerard (Donovan Leitch) and Andy (Jared Harris) in the Factory

© Chris Makos

Michael Imperioli as Ondine
© Joyce George, courtesy of Orion
Pictures Corporation

Myriam Cyr as Ultra Violet
© Joyce George, courtesy of Orion
Pictures Corporation

Victor Browne as Danny
© Joyce George, courtesy of Orion
Pictures Corporation

Christina McKay as Superstar #1
© Joyce George, courtesy of Orion
Pictures Corporation

Tahnee Welch as Viva
© Joyce George, courtesy of Orion
Pictures Corporation

Reg Rogers as Paul Morrissey
© Joyce George, courtesy of Orion
Pictures Corporation

Donovan Leitch as Gerard Malanga
© Joyce George, courtesy of Orion Pictures
Corporation

Coco McPherson as Bridget Berlin
© Joyce George, courtesy of Orion
Pictures Corporation

Stephen Dorff as Candy Darling
© Chris Makos

WARHOL

Oh, Valerie, you've written something—that's great.

BRIGID
(*looking at the first page*)
You dyke, you're disgusting.

BRIGID flounces off.

WARHOL
(*examining the manifesto*)
Did you type this yourself? I'm so impressed.

VALERIE
(*to* WARHOL)
So, are you going to produce my play? You should
do it now. It's going to cost you more when I'm
famous. A big-time publisher wants me to write a
novel, you know.

WARHOL
(*in his encouraging paternal mode*)
Oh, wow! That's great. Did you hear that, Viva?
Valerie's going to be published.

VIVA stares over Valerie's shoulder, bored.

VIVA
Really?

VALERIE
(*very much wanting to impress them*)
Yeah, Maurice Girodias. He's really famous. He's
French. He published Henry Miller and William
Burroughs and *Lolita* and all that high-class porn.
I'm in good, perverted company.

VIVA calls a friend over to sit beside her, and they begin to whisper, ignoring VALERIE.

CANDY saunters over and takes BRIGID's empty chair next to WARHOL.

> WARHOL
> (*introducing her to an attractive young
> man next to him*)
> Jason, this is Candy Darling.

> CANDY
> I'm calling myself Candy Warhol now . . . *cashing in*.

> WARHOL
> Look at Candy, Valerie—isn't she beautiful? Why
> don't you get her to do your makeup?

> VALERIE
> (*still badgering* WARHOL)
> So, are you going to produce my play?

> WARHOL
> Gee, Valerie, we're so busy right now.

> VALERIE
> Just give me an advance on it. I really need some
> money.

> WARHOL
> Valerie, get a job. Aren't you working anywhere?

> VALERIE
> Aw, Andy, you know that's against my principles.
> How about twenty bucks, just to get me through the
> week.

WARHOL

Okay. I've got a better idea. If you come over to the Factory tomorrow, you can be in our movie. That way you can earn the money instead of panhandling. We'll give you twenty-five dollars.

VALERIE

That's great, Andy. Can I have an advance?

WARHOL sighs.
A hand passes a rolled-up five dollar bill right into the camera's point of view—reminiscent of the shot of a gun barrel in the opening scene.

WARHOL

We've been wondering, Candy . . . how often do you get your period?

CANDY

Every day, Andy. I'm such a woman.

INTERIOR: THE FACTORY. DAY.

A corner of the Factory has been turned into an impromptu film studio with lights and equipment everywhere. VALERIE is standing in a corner, some distance behind WARHOL, who has his back to the camera. Every so often, he beckons to MORRISSEY and whispers in his ear; MORRISSEY then calls out his instructions to the actors. DANNY is on the film set.
TOM, a handsome young man with a bare chest and jeans, is standing in the middle of the set.
WARHOL whispers.

MORRISSEY

Okay, take off your pants.

Embarrassed, TOM does so.

> MORRISSEY
> Okay, put them back on.

WARHOL whispers.

> MORRISSEY
> Okay, turn around the other way and take them off
> again. We want to shoot it from a different angle.

IRIS, the high-strung, red-haired model, walks onto the set, dressed
in nothing but a pair of grubby bikini underpants.

> IRIS
> I hate the morning. Is this the morning?

IRIS notices what TOM is doing in front of the camera.

> IRIS
> (*screaming*)
> What is he *doing*? He's taking his pants off—I said I
> wouldn't do it if he took his pants off.

> TOM
> (*wrapping a towel around his waist*)
> Hey, it's okay. Be cool. I'll put them back on.

TOM goes behind the camera and begins to take off the towel to
put his jeans back on.

> IRIS
> He's taking his clothes off again!
> (*She turns to* MORRISSEY:)

This is all your fault, you cocksucker. You promised
me—

>   MORRISSEY
> Stop being hysterical.

WARHOL gestures to the cameraman to keep filming.
IRIS slaps Morrissey's face and runs into the other room, scream-
ing, "I am not hysterical!"
WARHOL looks on amused; he is enjoying this.

>   WARHOL
> I don't understand her. Iris'll cut her wrists for me,
> but she'll always go out of the frame or out of the
> room when I try and film it.

Sounds of screaming and objects smashing in the other room.
BILLY runs in and drags her out.

>   IRIS
> You can't do that to me. I am Mrs. Andy Warhol.
> You can't touch me. *Andy, help me please!!!*

They watch in silence as IRIS is dragged out of the room, screaming, "I am Mrs. Andy Warhol!"

>   WARHOL
> Uh, where's Valerie?

VALERIE is lurking, frightened, in the shadows.

>   MORRISSEY
> Okay, Valerie, you're on.

VALERIE comes forward hesitantly.

WARHOL

Don't try and act—just be yourself.

INTERIOR: FACTORY STAIRCASE. DAY.

Here, for the first and last time at the Factory, VALERIE is in the spotlight. Everyone else hovers in a circle of darkness around her, working the camera, adjusting the sound, standing in little groups watching.

Through the movie lights, we see VALERIE ascending the staircase with TOM, the actor from the previous scene. She stops when she reaches a doorway.

VALERIE

Uh, right here, this is the place.

TOM

Can I come in?

VALERIE

What am I doing up here with a finko like you?

TOM

Well, I thought we could, you know, talk and smoke, drink . . .

VALERIE

I can't figure it out—you're a fink.

TOM

You don't even know me.

VALERIE

Help me out, help me out—what is my motivation?
Oh, I remember: it all started in the elevator when I
grabbed your ass and squeezed it. It's real squishy.

How'd you get it so squishy? I mean, you got a
squishing machine?

TOM

It gets squeezed a lot, yeah. Can we go inside?

VALERIE

No—my roommate's in there, and by the way, she's
squishier than you.

TOM

Can't we just step inside your place for about a
minute?

VALERIE

I told you my roommate's in there. Look, I admit I
was weak. You got me at a weak moment; I mean,
I'm a pushover for a squishy ass. What else have ya
got?

TOM

I don't talk about those things, baby.

VALERIE

Give me one good reason why I should take you in
my pad.

TOM

We can discover . . . explore . . . we can explore one
another's heads, one another's bodies, you know . . .

VALERIE

Look, I've got the upper hand. We must not forget
that.

Strobe cut.

> VALERIE
>
> Look, man, this *conversation* is getting to be a drag.

Strobe cut.

> TOM
>
> Babe, my hang-up is that you're sitting here, telling me that you don't even want to talk.

> VALERIE
>
> What talk? I squished your ass, you mean.

> TOM
>
> You see, you're making aggressive moves, that's where you're at. You just wanted to set up this whole situation, didn't you?

> VALERIE
>
> You took it the wrong way. I don't live here; I just came here to beat my meat.

> TOM
>
> Wait a minute, you *started* . . . you . . . I'm not going to stop, forget it.

VALERIE walks down the staircase.

> VALERIE
>
> Come on, man. I wanna go home. I wanna beat my meat.

> MORRISSEY
>
> Cut!

SUSAN and BILLY applaud.

> WARHOL
> Valerie, that was *so* great . . .

INTERIOR: WARHOL'S DESK, THE FACTORY. DAY.

WARHOL is sitting at his desk, holding the phone away as he turns to slurp some vegetable soup with a spoon.

INTERIOR: VALERIE'S ROOM, CHELSEA HOTEL. DAY.

> VALERIE
> Christ, a snake couldn't live on what you pay out.

INTERIOR: WARHOL'S DESK, THE FACTORY. DAY.

WARHOL takes another spoonful of soup.

INTERIOR: VALERIE'S ROOM, CHELSEA HOTEL. DAY.

> VALERIE
> *Hello?* . . . And while you're at it, I need that play back.

> WARHOL
> (*voice-over*)
> Oh, Valerie, I'm sorry about your script. I don't know where it is . . . people give us so many things, I can't keep track . . .

VALERIE

Andy, I *need* it; I want to show it to my publisher. I've only got one other copy, and I don't want to give him mine. I'm having dinner with him tonight—he's taking me to El Quixote.

INTERIOR: WARHOL'S DESK, THE FACTORY. DAY.

WARHOL

Oh, how glamorous! Wear makeup. You're kind of pale, so you should wear a lot of blush.

INTERIOR: CANDY'S ROOM, HOTEL EARLE. NIGHT.

The screen is black. A radio is playing in the background; then we hear Candy's voice.

CANDY
(*offscreen*)

Look up. Open your eyes!

Valerie's point of view: CANDY is looming over her, mascara wand in hand.
VALERIE is sitting in the bathroom, on the edge of the toilet. The room is all white tile.

CANDY

Hold still!

CANDY very gently brushes mascara onto Valerie's lower lashes. In a close-up, we see the mascara wand descending toward Valerie's point of view. VALERIE flinches slightly.

CANDY
Almost done.

VALERIE
Thank God.

CANDY
So, what's he like, this Frenchman—is he attractive?

VALERIE
How should I know? This is business, not a romance.

Disappointed, CANDY tilts Valerie's head back and brandishes the
mascara at her.

CANDY
Open your eyes. And don't move.

Helpless, VALERIE obeys. CANDY begins stroking mascara onto
Valerie's upper lashes.
She pushes Valerie's head back and examines VALERIE's face.

CANDY
Go like this.

CANDY purses her lips. VALERIE imitates her.

CANDY
Now for my secret weapon.

CANDY brings out a lipstick and unscrews it. From Valerie's point
of view, an extreme close-up of the lipstick moving toward her.

CANDY
Revlon's Fire and Ice.

VALERIE closes her eyes.
Cut to VALERIE and CANDY standing by the closet. VALERIE looks
startlingly different with makeup and looks attractive in her own,
odd way. CANDY rummages around the clothes and pulls out a pale
blue, beaded gown.

> CANDY
>
> How about this?

> VALERIE
>
> Christ, no.
>   (CANDY *looks offended.*)
> Haven't you got something more . . . dignified? This
> is an important dinner for me.

CANDY sighs, rustles in the closet, and brings out a scarlet sheath.
VALERIE looks approving.

> VALERIE
>
> Let's try that one.

CANDY floats a large scarf over Valerie's head to protect her hair
and makeup, slips the red dress over her head, and zips her up in
back. VALERIE examines herself in the mirror.

> VALERIE
>
> Yeah, I think I could wear this. On my way to a date
> with destiny.

EXTERIOR: NEW YORK CITY STREETS. NIGHT.

VALERIE hurries across town in the red dress. She carries her own
clothes in a stained brown-paper bag.

INTERIOR: EL QUIXOTE RESTAURANT. NIGHT.

GIRODIAS is waiting at a table. He stands up to greet VALERIE as she arrives.
He is obviously startled to see her in Candy's glamorous red dress.

> VALERIE
> (*gruffly*)
> Don't you think I'm a good-looking girl?

> GIRODIAS
> I'm overcome. What a contract will do for a woman!

GIRODIAS motions to a WAITER, lights Valerie's cigarette.
Close-up, flame approaching Valerie's point of view.
Girodias pours her champagne.

> GIRODIAS
> (*voice-over*)
> People will very soon tire of the vulgar sex fiction of the last few years. A new form of erotic literature is going to emerge from the dungheap of pornography, and I am the publisher to provide it . . .

We jump cut through the following conversation, punctuating the argument with images from the meal and the surrounding restaurant. A flamenco guitarist plays a seductive tune throughout.
The WAITER delivers two huge lobsters to their table.

> VALERIE
> So I said to Andy, "Can't you see all the groovy projects that SCUM has to offer?"

> GIRODIAS
>
> Well, you know, I am a passionate feminist myself . . .

Cut to VALERIE holding up a claw and examining it as if she were back in the lab. GIRODIAS takes it from her and shows her how to open it. They are both wearing lobster bibs.

> GIRODIAS
>
> I agree with you that men have been bad and stu-pid—look at this insane all-male Vietnam War. But are women really any better?

Cut to VALERIE cracking open a claw.

> VALERIE
>
> There have been no female revolutionaries because there have been no true females, only brainwashed cows. Can't you see what the world would be like if the real soul sisters took over?

> GIRODIAS
>
> Prove it to me.

Cut to the WAITER refilling their wine glasses.

> VALERIE
> (*slightly drunk*)
>
> I'm going to take all the money I get and buy a bus, call it the Scumnibus—and drive around the coun-try recruiting followers for SCUM.

Cut to GIRODIAS offering a toast to VALERIE.

> GIRODIAS
> (*even more drunk*)

I expect to make a million dollars in the next six months. Soon you will have the pleasure of knowing a new Girodias, an opulent Girodias, with a gardenia in his buttonhole and a greyhound as white as snow at his feet, a fifty dollar cigar between his lips . . .

Cut to the remains of dessert.

> VALERIE
> So, let's get this straight . . . I get five hundred now and another five hundred when I deliver the manuscript and the rest when it's published. That's it?

> GIRODIAS
> It's as simple as that.

Close-up of the contract lying on the white tablecloth. GIRODIAS hands VALERIE a black fountain pen. She signs the contract. He passes her a check for five hundred dollars. She holds it up to the light, as if she can't believe it's real.

INTERIOR: VALERIE'S ROOM, CHELSEA HOTEL. DAY.

On the desk a typewriter with a piece of paper blank except for the words VALERIE SOLANAS.
Close-up of a very long cigarette ash trembling at the end of a cigarette.
VALERIE is motionless at her desk, staring at the contract, her lips moving as she reads:

> VALERIE
> "The rights to all European territories shall be granted in perpetuity" . . . what the fuck does that *mean*?

The ash falls into the typewriter keys.
VALERIE puts the contract down and stares at the wall.

> VALERIE
>
> What have I done?

INTERIOR: THE FACTORY. DAY.

The sound of a match striking as ONDINE lights a cigarette, lying on the floor. He is surrounded by a little group of hangers-on, including ROTTEN RITA, who is busy scribbling in her trip book. VALERIE and WARHOL sit on the couch. She is studying her Girodias contract, which is now even more crumpled, folded into squares. WARHOL is on the telephone, listening intently to the voice on the other end. In one hand, he holds a microphone, which he points at VALERIE, but otherwise, he ignores her.

> WARHOL
>
> He *did?* . . . You *are?* . . . She *was?* . . . *Ohhh* . . .

> VALERIE
>
> (*reading from the contract*)
>
> "A rate of 6 percent on the first twenty thousand copies"
>
> (*looking up and addressing the microphone*)
>
> I signed this contract with that low toad, Girodias, and now, he's got me all tied up. But I don't wanna write a novel. I wanna publish the "SCUM Manifesto" instead, but Girodias doesn't have the balls. If he's so radical, why won't he publish SCUM?

A couple of young girls enter from the elevator and, giggling, walk past ONDINE and his friends and seek out GERARD.
ONDINE watches them from the couch.

ONDINE

Danny, tell Gerard to stop bringing those tacky creatures up here . . . just tell him don't bring all those
fucky girls up here because they make us feel like
creatures in a zoo.

DANNY

Tell him yourself.

ONDINE
(*sadly, addressing the others*)
Danny doesn't care about my dick. I mean, I don't
want to answer for you, Danny. If you'd like to see
it and hold it and know it as your own you can, I'll
be very gentle . . .

Distracted by the sound of shouting across the room, ONDINE
glances over at VALERIE, who is talking excitedly.

VALERIE

So there are *two* aspects to SCUM—the destructive
and the constructive, destroying the old world
through sabotage and beginning to create a swinging, out-of-sight female world.

ONDINE

Oh, what is that crazy bitch going on about now?

Cut to VALERIE and WARHOL on the couch.

VALERIE

You see, that's the answer!

WARHOL
(*on the phone*)
Okay, call me right back.

VALERIE

You could publish it—why not? SCUM could crack
this whole country wide open.

WARHOL

Oh, Valerie, I'm not a publisher.

VALERIE
(*not listening, as she gets up and paces around
with a cigarette in her hand*)
You could be part of the organization! I'm starting
a men's auxiliary, and you could be the head of it.
Of course, I'd still make all the key decisions . . .

WARHOL stares at her blankly.

VALERIE
(*excited*)
Listen, if you put all your assets, past and future, into
a SCUM fund, I'll do the same.
(*A note of doubt enters her voice as she senses
his lack of enthusiasm for this idea:*)
Oh, Andy, don't you see how groovy it could be?
America is crying, dying for a change. The whole
world is.

The phone rings. WARHOL picks it up on the first ring.

WARHOL
(*ignoring her*)
Hi . . . you are? . . . Really, he is? . . .

VALERIE walks away, disappointed.
ONDINE watches her from the floor.

> ONDINE
> (*addressing the hangers-on*)
> Listen, we have to start instituting rules here. Noth-
> ing but the best-looking women are allowed in here
> . . . and *without* cunts.

VALERIE stops, wheels round, and heads back to ONDINE. She hands
him a copy of the manifesto.

> VALERIE
> Did you know that males are biologically inferior
> females? Maybe you should read this.

> ONDINE
> (*tossing it away*)
> I don't want your tacky writing. What makes you
> think Andy wants to publish you?

VALERIE is silent.

> ONDINE
> What makes you think that Andy Warhol—the great-
> est living artist of our time—would want to publish
> the ravings of a lunatic? I'm just curious.

VALERIE crouches down, so her face is on Ondine's level.

> VALERIE
> I'm not a lunatic, asshole. I'm a revolutionary. There
> are thousands of women behind me. I have a whole
> lot of followers and we have seen the future and we
> will inherit the fucking Earth . . .

Close on Ondine's face.

INTERIOR: THE FACTORY. DAY.

VALERIE paces back and forth by the table where WARHOL and FRED HUGHES are working, looking through still photographs for the Death and Disaster series. They try to ignore her, barely looking up as she talks to them. Her monologue has clearly been going on for some time.

> VALERIE
>
> So the guy has no money, right? After I give him the book, that'll be it. I'm now hip to what Girodias's greasy contract means. I sold the novel outright— the only right I have is to the royalties, which I'm sure he'll find a way of beating me out of and—

> FRED
> (*trying to shut her up*)
> Oh, just give him a blow job.

> WARHOL
>
> Write a novel on file cards. Then you can give him a book a day.

> MORRISSEY
> (*without looking up from his desk*)
> Have yourself committed to a mental institution in order to frustrate him.
> (*Sarcastically:*)
> They'll *never* look for you there.

Close on Valerie's burning face. They seem oblivious to how deeply upset she is.

VALERIE
Well, you can join me there, you fag bastard.

The men look at each other—she has gone too far.

VALERIE
You think you can treat me like shit, just because I'm
a woman and you're a bunch of fags!

VALERIE seizes the table in front of them and knocks it over,
spilling slides, ashtrays, artwork, plastic cups of soda onto the
ground.
The men stare in horror as the soda seeps over the color slides.

WARHOL
Billy!!

BILLY rushes over. He puts his arm around Valerie's shoulders,
firmly leading her away.

BILLY
I'm sorry, Valerie. You have to leave now.

BILLY marches VALERIE away from WARHOL. The camera follows
them as they slowly walk the length of the Factory, past artworks
and blown-up photos and some random Factory activity, leaving
WARHOL and the others to recede in the distance.

VALERIE
(*voice-over*)
The male "artist" attempts to solve his dilemma of
not being able to live, of not being female, by constructing a highly artificial world in which the male
is heroized . . .

MANIFESTO SEQUENCE.

> VALERIE
>
> We know that "great art" is great, because male au-
> thorities have told us so, and we can't claim other-
> wise, as only those with exquisite sensibilities far
> superior to ours can appreciate the greatness, the
> proof of their superior sensitivity being that they
> appreciate the slop that they appreciate . . .

INTERIOR: CHELSEA HOTEL LOBBY. DAY.

The MANAGER is bending over the camera, which is Valerie's point
of view.

> MANAGER
>
> Miss Solanas, I have had many complaints about you
> harassing the other guests. And I must warn you that
> if you do not pay your rent—

VALERIE is sitting bolt upright on her usual bench, staring at people
wandering in and out.

> VALERIE
> (*emotionless*)
> Fuck off, you little creep. Where's Girodias? I need
> to see him.

VALERIE continues to stare blankly in front of her. There are tears
in her eyes.

> GIRODIAS
> (*offscreen*)
> Valerie? Are you all right?

VALERIE
They're gonna throw me out. I need fifty bucks.

GIRODIAS
(*sighing, annoyed—we see him looking down
into Valerie's point of view*)
I only have ten. You do realize, Valerie, that I paid
you five hundred dollars six months ago, and I have
not seen one line of your novel?

VALERIE
These things take time.

GIRODIAS
What about your Mr. Warhol? Maybe he'll put you
in another film.

VALERIE
Talking to him is like talking to a chair. And he still
has my script, and he won't give it back. I think he
wants to steal it—make a movie of *my* script and not
give me any credit. I know Warhol has front groups,
that he's an invisible partner in a lot of enterprises . . .

GIRODIAS
(*putting a ten dollar bill in her hand*)
Write the book, my dear. Get to work.

INTERIOR: MAX'S KANSAS CITY. NIGHT.
VALERIE stands at the entrance to Max's backroom. The owner
stands in front of her to prevent her coming in. WARHOL and a
small entourage wander out. VALERIE steps up to WARHOL and
touches his arm as he shrinks away.

> VALERIE
> Andy, please, I gotta talk to you . . . it's important.

> WARHOL
> (*backing away*)
> Oh hi, Val. We were just leaving. Salvador Dalí's
> having a party tonight at the St. Regis.
> (*A pause as she looks at him expectantly.*)
> I'm sorry we can't take you with us.

WARHOL rushes away, followed by the others, except for ONDINE, who pauses for a moment by VALERIE, who is staring after WARHOL.

> ONDINE
> Don't you get it? You've been excommunicated,
> honey.

ONDINE makes a cross over VALERIE and then walks away.

EXTERIOR: PHONE BOOTH. EVENING.

VALERIE is standing at a phone booth across the street from the Factory.

> VALERIE
> This is Valerie Solanas. I gotta speak to Andy.

From the street, she can look up at the windows of the Factory. Every few seconds, the windows are illuminated by a flash of light, then darkness again, as if there were an electrical storm going on inside.

> VALERIE
> (*plaintive*)
> *Why* can't he speak to me?

INTERIOR: THE FACTORY. EVENING.

A photo shoot is in progress. A huge white cyc has been placed against one wall, and one by one, the Factory stars are posing against the white background, under bright lights. As the camera flashes blindingly, we see these images:

BRIGID, naked to the waist, scowling.

VIVA looking enigmatic.

GERARD posing.

CANDY vamping.

DANNY shooting; WARHOL directing.

> VALERIE
> (*offscreen*)
> S-O-L-A-N-A-S . . . "Up Your Ass" . . .

EXTERIOR: PHONE BOOTH. EVENING.

> VALERIE
> What's going on? . . . I don't know who you are either, jerk. Tell him I want that script. Or else.

VALERIE hangs up. She stands in the street looking up at the lights flashing in the Factory windows.

INTERIOR: UNDERGROUND NEWSPAPER OFFICE. DAY.

Title on screen: SPRING 1968.

Close-up of a mimeograph machine spewing out copies. Valerie's hand reaches in to collect the copies. Close on what is being printed: the title page of the "SCUM Manifesto."

VALERIE is standing in the offices of the *East Village Other* underground newspaper. The walls are covered with posters advocating Latin American or Chinese revolution or advertising concerts, and personal notices.

MARK MOTHERFUCKER and REVOLUTIONARY NUMBER ONE and REVO-
LUTIONARY NUMBER TWO—three good-looking, long-haired boys
in heavy work boots, dungarees, and combat jackets—are on the
other side of the room, watching her. They have piles of leaflets
in their hands. They look at each other and then approach.

> MARK
> (*handing her a leaflet*)
> Here, take this. We're having an action tomorrow.
> We're going to dump garbage all over Lincoln Center.

> VALERIE
> (*deadpan*)
> Groovy. You call that an *action?*

> REVOLUTIONARY
> (*offended*)
> Yeah, man. We're going to bury bourgeois culture
> in shit.

MARK reaches over and grabs a copy of the "SCUM Manifesto."
VALERIE grabs it back and gives him an unwavering stare.

> VALERIE
> Fifty cents.

Reluctantly, MARK digs into his pocket and hands her fifty cents.
She hands him a copy of the manifesto.

> MARK
> We're the Motherfuckers.

> REVOLUTIONARY
> We're, like, a street gang with an analysis.

MARK
(*scanning the manifesto*)
So—how long have you been in this SCUM bag?

INTERIOR: LOWER EAST SIDE APARTMENT. DAY.

The bedroom of Mark's chaotic tenement apartment. It is strewn with piles of laundry, books, papers, empty bottles, overflowing ashtrays, revolutionary posters, combat gear. On one wall is a poster showing a hand holding a revolver, pointed straight at the viewer, and the slogan WE'RE LOOKING FOR PEOPLE WHO LIKE TO DRAW. Above the bed is painted another slogan, ARMED LOVE.
The following conversation takes place in a series of jump or strobe cuts, as if the conversation had been roughly edited, as VALERIE and MARK lecture each other on their political beliefs.
Music for this sequence: the Jimi Hendrix version of "Wild Thing," or an instrumental version as close to Hendrix as possible.
Half-dressed, standing on the bed, MARK poses with a machine gun in front of VALERIE.

MARK
We're against everything that's "good and decent" in honky America. We will burn and loot and destroy. We are the incubation of your mother's nightmare.

Cut to MARK showing VALERIE his ammunition belt.

MARK
You don't begin to be free until your own blood is being shed at the end of a baton.

VALERIE takes the belt and wraps it around herself as she delivers her lecture.

> VALERIE
>
> SCUM, being cool and selfish, will not subject itself
> to getting rapped on the head with billy clubs; that's
> for the nice "privileged, educated" middle class . . .

Strobe cuts of VALERIE and MARK as they strike various militant poses
around the room—voguing for revolutionaries—playing with
combat gear and the contents of Mark's weapons chest.

> VALERIE
>
> SCUM will not picket, demonstrate, march, or strike
> to attempt to achieve its ends. If SCUM ever
> marches, it will be over the president's stupid, sick-
> ening face; if SCUM ever strikes, it will be in the dark
> with a six-inch blade.

Strobe cuts of VALERIE and MARK making out awkwardly on the
bed.
Cut to VALERIE lying on her stomach on the bed, smoking. MARK
lies half on top of her.

> MARK
> (*reminiscing*)
> We were in this airplane, and we went up and down
> the aisle borrowing food from people's plates. They
> didn't know we were revolutionaries. They just knew
> we were *crazy*. That's what we're about—being crazy
> motherfuckers and scaring the shit out of honky
> America.

> VALERIE
> (*bored, looking round the room*)
> How much do you pay for this place anyway?

Strobe cuts of more banal sex action.

VALERIE

Do you need a roommate? I don't have any money
for rent, but I could fuck you sometimes.

Strobe cuts of more sex action.

INTERIOR: LOWER EAST SIDE APARTMENT. NIGHT.

MARK is fast asleep. VALERIE is sitting up in bed in the dark, wide
awake, staring. Her eyes are fixed on the poster of the gun on the
opposite wall.

INTERIOR: LOWER EAST SIDE APARTMENT. THE NEXT MORNING.

MARK is still asleep in the bed. VALERIE is dressed and quietly going
through the pockets of his jeans. She pulls out three cents and
contemptuously pockets them. She opens a drawer and riffles
through it. She pulls out a handful of bullets.
She goes over to the weapons chest, rummages through it, and
pulls out a silver handgun.
VALERIE holds the gun in her hand, turning it over. She points it
straight at the mirror and holds a pose, staring at her reflection,
in the style of the poster on the wall.

EXTERIOR: STREET CORNER. NIGHT.

VALERIE stands on the corner, offering her manifesto to everyone
who walks by. Most people brush past without even looking at
her. Finally, a DISINTERESTED GIRL stops.

DISINTERESTED GIRL

What's this?

>   VALERIE
>   (*shy, almost embarrassed*)
> It's something I wrote.

VALERIE keeps thrusting it toward the DISINTERESTED GIRL.

>   DISINTERESTED GIRL
>   Okay, okay. How much?

>   VALERIE
> For you, twenty-five cents. It's a dollar for men.

VALERIE searches for change but finds nothing.

>   DISINTERESTED GIRL
>   Sorry.

>   VALERIE
>   Take one anyway.

>   DISINTERESTED GIRL
>   (*walking off*)
>   No, that's okay.

VALERIE stands as if frozen on the corner, holding out a copy of the manifesto, ignored by passersby.

INTERIOR: CANDY'S ROOM, HOTEL EARLE. DAY.

Close-up of a television screen.
First, image of the 1968 Miss America contest, as the contestants come onstage, displaying their gowns.

>   CANDY
>   (*offscreen*)
> Balenciaga.

> VALERIE
> (*offscreen*)

Bitch. Slave.

Another contestant swirls on.

> CANDY
> (*offscreen*)

Givenchy.

> VALERIE
> (*offscreen*)

Toadie. Sycophant.

Another girl swirls on.
Cut to CANDY in curlers and hairnet.

> CANDY

No, Dior.

> VALERIE

Whore.

Wide shot of Candy's bed, where CANDY, JEREMIAH, and VALERIE are watching the television.

> CANDY

She should be wearing black. Black is perfect for the evening, as well as for daytime wear. A girl always looks good in black.
> (*She shifts into the mode of a television announcer:*)
> Black—the color of choice.

The television screen is suddenly invaded by images of protesting women disrupting the Miss America contest.
CANDY, JEREMIAH, and VALERIE are astonished by what is on screen.

CANDY

Oh, my God! . . . I find all these social protests very
disturbing . . . all these revolutionary girls come
across very hard to me, and I don't like hardness,
especially in women.

VALERIE
(*exasperated*)
Oh, Jesus, Candy.

Close on television: more newsreel footage of the protest.
VALERIE paces back and forth in front of the television, muttering
to herself.

VALERIE

These women got everything from me. The "SCUM
Manifesto" is the most revolutionary document ever
written.

CANDY
You're blocking my view.

VALERIE
I should be there.

CANDY
Please be quiet, Valerie. I want to see this. This is
history.

VALERIE
I should be there. Why doesn't anyone put *me* on
TV?

JEREMIAH
I can get you on TV.

VALERIE looks at him skeptically.

> JEREMIAH
> A friend of my sister works on the Alan Burke show.

INTERIOR: BACKSTAGE, *ALAN BURKE SHOW*. DAY.

In the background, we can see VALERIE swathed in an apron, leaning back helpless in a barber's chair as a MAKEUP GIRL slaps white Pan-Cake all over Valerie's face.

In the foreground, ALISON, a young researcher with a clipboard, is conferring with JEREMIAH.

> ALISON
> Sweetie, we have a bit of a problem. The other dykes—I mean, women—have backed down. But don't worry. Alan says he's a big fan of Valerie's writing, and he's really looking forward to meeting her.

INTERIOR: ALAN BURKE STUDIO. DAY.

The television show is in progress. VALERIE and ALAN BURKE, a mean, little man in his fifties with a goatee beard, sit under the white glare of television lights. He smokes continuously throughout the show.

BURKE adopts a supercilious and aggressively sarcastic tone. He is confrontational to the point of self-parody, baiting his guests for the audience's amusement.

Alan Burke Show theme music plays in background. Applause.

> BURKE
> Although I've read in the newspapers about homosexuals, and according to the Kinsey report, there

must be one under every rock, I find it rather *repul-sive* that they are now seeking social acceptance . . .

Cut to black-and-white viewfinder of an old-fashioned studio camera.
Camera tracks in to a tight close-up of BURKE.

> BURKE
> (*continuing*)
> This was supposed to be a show about *women* homo-sexuals. Lesbians. And the gals we got chickened out—but here before me is one that didn't chicken out. And why?

BURKE and VALERIE are onstage under the bright studio lights. Silhouetted studio technicians wander back and forth in front of the monitor screen.

> BURKE
> Because she has her own ax to grind. And, boy, ladies and gentlemen, did she pick the wrong place to grind it!

Sound effect of a lion roaring. In the foreground, a sound technician operating the effect.

> BURKE
> Valerie—that's your name, isn't it?

Close-up on VALERIE stunned by the noise and bright lights, not knowing what to say. Her face is white with Pan-Cake makeup; her cheeks are spots of red: she looks like a deranged clown.

> VALERIE
> Yes, it is.

> BURKE

Well, Valerie, I understand that you're a lesbian—a
somewhat *mannish* one at that. Whatsamatter . . .
didn't anyone ever take you to the prom?

The audience members hoot.
Valerie's face is growing redder under her layers of makeup.

> VALERIE

Who cares? Look, Alan, I am here for one reason
and one reason only—to discuss the oppression of
women for thousands of years by men.

Two technicians crouch, watching. They grin at each other, shaking their heads.
Cut to close-up of JEREMIAH, looking anxious.

> VALERIE

If you look at the history of oppression, it was always
men who caused the problems. Men who caused
wars. Men who raped, pillaged, and destroyed. If you
look back, you'll—

In the background, hostile murmurs from the audience.

> BURKE

I think the studio audience gets the drift, Valerie.

VALERIE is now sweating under the lights, the powder on her face
streaking. The hostile murmurs are growing louder.

> VALERIE
> (*nonplussed by all this hostility*)

If you look at Vietnam, you'll see a series of—

AUDIENCE MEMBER
(*offscreen*)
Communist!

BURKE
Isn't it true that you'd stop at nothing to undermine American values and mores? And isn't it true that you're just a pathetic excuse for a woman? I've seen creatures in the zoo that had more class than you.

VALERIE
Alan, control yourself. Let's not get personal.

By now the audience is shrieking.
BURKE stands up to display VALERIE to the audience.

BURKE
I ask you, ladies and gentlemen, have you ever heard anything as sick and perverted as this woman?

VALERIE
Alan, try to control yourself. Try not to show the public what a scumbag you really are.

BURKE
Did you hear what she said? She called me a *scumbag*.
(*He pronounces the word slowly, as if
hearing it for the first time.*)
That's it. Call the lions out.
(*Turning to the floor manager:*)
Throw this cunt off the set.

Cut to VALERIE. She sits there, tears of rage in her eyes, her face getting redder and redder, squeezing the arms of the chair so hard her knuckles are white.

Cut to JEREMIAH with his head in his hands.

The audience's shrieks are now mixed with the tape of the lion roaring over and over, as if the tape is stuck.

VALERIE stands up, takes the chair, and tries to smash it over Burke's head, as he dances out of the way.

> DIRECTOR
>
> *Cut! Cut!*

The two technicians rush out of frame. Security guards and several men from the audience run onto the stage. The sound effects guy joins them, forgetting to switch off his machine, so the lion roars over and over.

There is a struggle as the men pin VALERIE to her chair. They seize and carry her out of the studio, arms and legs flailing wildly.

INTERIOR: CANDY'S ROOM, HOTEL EARLE. DAY.

VALERIE is in the middle of a vicious fight with JEREMIAH. CANDY cowers in the corner, horrified. VALERIE has JEREMIAH pinned down on the bed and is twisting his arm behind his hack.

> VALERIE
>
> *You set me up!* Who told you to set me up?

VALERIE twists Jeremiah's arm behind his back until he whimpers in pain.

> VALERIE
>
> Was it Andy? Did Andy tell you to do it?

> JEREMIAH
> (*in tears, hardly able to speak*)
> No one . . . no one told me anything.

Behind them, CANDY has crept over to the phone and is dialing.

> CANDY
> Operator—call the police, it's an—

VALERIE jumps off the bed and knocks the phone out of Candy's hand. JEREMIAH, released, runs out the door.
VALERIE slaps CANDY across the face.

> VALERIE
> Were you in on it too, you little toady? Sucking up
> to Andy?

CANDY collapses on the bed, weeping.

> VALERIE
> You think he likes you? He likes you 'cause he hates
> women and you're a freak!

VALERIE sweeps her hand across Candy's immaculate dressing table, knocking off makeup, costume jewelry, and perfume bottles, which shatter on the floor.

> VALERIE
> You're not a woman, *Jimmy*. You're not a man.
> You're just pathetic.

INTERIOR: OLYMPIA PRESS OFFICES. DAY.

GIRODIAS is in the middle of a meeting with one of his authors, CECIL—a small, plump man with black spectacles and a struggling moustache.

> GIRODIAS
> (*indicating the manuscript in front of him*)
> Have you decided on a title?

CECIL
"Sea of Thighs."

GIRODIAS
(*nodding with approval*)
I enjoyed this. It's an amusing study of nympho-
mania and marital cannibalism.
(*The telephone rings.*)
Excuse me.

GIRODIAS picks up the receiver.

EXTERIOR: STREET CORNER PHONE BOOTH. DAY.

VALERIE is calling GIRODIAS. As she talks, she is playing with an ice
pick, scratching at the metal of the booth.

VALERIE
Hello, toad. I know it was you who set me up on
that TV show.

INTERIOR: OLYMPIA PRESS OFFICES. DAY.

GIRODIAS gestures to CECIL that this will only take a moment.

GIRODIAS
(*to* VALERIE)
What TV show? I'm in a meeting at the moment.
Perhaps we can discuss this later.

EXTERIOR: STREET CORNER PHONE BOOTH. DAY.

>   VALERIE
> I'm going to cut your balls off and stick them down
> your throat.

INTERIOR: OLYMPIA PRESS OFFICES. DAY.

>   GIRODIAS
>   (*unflappable*)
> Yes, we'll talk later. Thank you so much for calling.
>   (*He puts the receiver down and stares into*
>   *space for a moment.*)
> Where was I? Oh yes. I'd like you to put in some
> more, really *outspoken* sex scenes . . .

>   CECIL
> Gang bangs, bestiality?

>   GIRODIAS
>   (*airily*)
> That sort of thing. I'd like you to do a book every
> two months . . .

EXTERIOR: STREET CORNER PHONE BOOTH. DAY.

VALERIE has gone. Close in on what she was writing with the ice
pick—SCUM.

INTERIOR: CHELSEA HOTEL CORRIDOR. DAY.

VALERIE walks down the corridor, muttering to herself. She reaches
the door, unlocks it, and swings it open. Inside her room, the

MANAGER, the BELL BOY and two policemen are waiting for her.
VALERIE and the others stare at each other for a moment, frozen.

INTERIOR: CHELSEA HOTEL LOBBY. DAY.
VALERIE is dragged screaming out of the lobby by the police. A
policeman grabs her, and she bites his hand hard. She clings fe-
rociously to her favorite bench as they pull on her legs to force
her to loosen her grip.

> VALERIE
> (*spitting*)
> *Get off me, you pig!*

VALERIE lets go, and they drag her wailing, along the ground:

> VALERIE
> *My stuff! I need my stuff!*

INTERIOR: THE FACTORY. DAY.
The old Factory is being dismantled. There are packing crates
everywhere, and assistants are carrying out the big silk screens,
wrapped in plastic.
ONDINE lies defiantly on the red sofa, smoking a cigarette.
Across the room MORRISSEY makes a contemptuous gesture toward
ONDINE and he mutters something to DANNY, who then approaches
the couch.

> DANNY
> Uh, Paul says if you're going to hang around here,
> you have to help us pack.

> ONDINE
> I refuse to take part in the destruction of something
> beautiful, just to satisfy *his* tawdry ambitions.

The phone rings.

> DANNY
> Aw, come on, Ondine. The new office is great.

> ONDINE
> Andy Warhol is an artist. He doesn't work in an *office*.

The phone keeps ringing. DANNY runs to answer it.

> DANNY
> Hello, Warhol Studios?

DANNY listens for a moment and then cups his hand over the receiver.

> DANNY
> It's Valerie again.

Exasperated, FRED HUGHES takes the phone.

> FRED
> I'm sorry, but Andy's in Paris right now . . .

DANNY holds the receiver away from his ear; there is screaming on the other end.

> VALERIE
> (*offscreen*)
> I need that script! Don't you understand? I haven't
> got another copy. I need it. Tell Andy I have a lot of
> followers now. If he doesn't give it back to me, they
> know what to do.

DANNY wanders over to the other end of the loft, where GERARD is packing up boxes. We hear the first part of the conversation from across the room, in voice-over.

DANNY
(*offscreen*)
So what's with Billy? I hear he locked himself in the
darkroom and won't come out.

GERARD
(*offscreen*)
I don't know, man. He freaked out. Can't handle
the new regime.

Cut to DANNY with a pile of papers in his arms.

DANNY
What do I do with this shit? Put it in the garbage?

GERARD
No, put it in a box. You know Andy can't bear to
throw anything away.

DANNY dumps the papers in an open packing crate.
Close on the crate. Partly visible among the papers is the bright
red cover of "Up Your Ass."
Another pile of papers is thrown in the box, covering the script.

EXTERIOR: PANHANDLING STREET CORNER.
EARLY EVENING.

Twilight. VALERIE is back on her usual panhandling street, stopping passersby, offering the manifesto, being rebuffed, swearing
at them. The street is littered with discarded copies of the manifesto, swirling in the wind.

INTERIOR: GIRODIAS'S ROOM, CHELSEA
HOTEL. NIGHT.

The phone rings in the dark; GIRODIAS grapples for it.

> GIRODIAS
> (*half asleep*)
Hello?

EXTERIOR: PHONE BOOTH. NIGHT.

> VALERIE
Are you sleeping?

INTERIOR: GIRODIAS'S ROOM, CHELSEA HOTEL. NIGHT.

> GIRODIAS
> (*struggling in the dark to find a light switch*)
What time is it?

The table lamp switches on, illuminating GIRODIAS in his pajamas. Beside him, with her back to the camera, a dark-haired woman shifts in her sleep.

EXTERIOR: PHONE BOOTH. NIGHT.
VALERIE is huddled, shivering, in a phone booth, on a deserted street corner.

> VALERIE
It's kinda late. Look, I'm out here on the corner—

> GIRODIAS
> (*offscreen*)
It's 4 A.M.

> VALERIE

I've got nowhere to stay. You've got a big apartment.
I'm really broke right now. I need to move in with
you for a few days.

INTERIOR: GIRODIAS'S ROOM, CHELSEA HOTEL. NIGHT.

> GIRODIAS

Jesus Christ.

The phone slams down. The light switches off.
The phone starts ringing again.

INTERIOR: HALLWAY OUTSIDE CANDY'S ROOM, HOTEL EARLE. NIGHT.

VALERIE is banging on Candy's door. Under her arm, VALERIE holds
a brown paper bag.

> VALERIE

Come on, Candy, open up! Candy, are you there? I
gotta talk to you!

Cut to CANDY behind the door, her eyes closed in terror, shaking.

INTERIOR: HALLWAY OUTSIDE STEVIE'S ROOM, CHEAP HOTEL. NIGHT.

Valerie's fist is banging on a door.

> VALERIE

Stevie, let me in!!

Cut to the door opening. STEVIE stands there, in a T-shirt and boxer shorts.

> STEVIE
>
> What the fuck? . . .

INTERIOR: STEVIE'S ROOM, CHEAP HOTEL. NIGHT.

STEVIE is asleep in the single bed. VALERIE is huddled up in a blanket on the floor, lit by moonlight or the streetlight from outside. She has a half-smoked cigarette in her hand. The ashtray is filled with cigarette butts. VALERIE is in midmonologue and has obviously been talking for some time.

> VALERIE
>
> And that's why Girodias won't print the manifesto until he makes me sign another contract, because he's already sold Andy the film rights behind my back.

Close on STEVIE, sound asleep, her mouth open, snoring gently.

> VALERIE
>
> Andy already has the play. I'll never be free of them. They have everything.

VALERIE brings out her new gun and looks at it gleaming in the dark. She points it at the camera, cocks the trigger, and aims it at STEVIE.
Stevie's eyes open. She shrinks back against the wall, staring at VALERIE. Slowly, VALERIE puts down the gun.

> STEVIE
>
> You're crazy. Get out of here, or I'll call the cops.

VALERIE

I wasn't trying to—

STEVIE

Get out! Get out! *Get out!*

EXTERIOR: NEW YORK STREETS. NIGHT.

VALERIE running headlong through the streets at night, clutching a brown paper bag. This is reminiscent of the early scene where she ran to meet Girodias, but the music is more sinister and the streets deserted.

EXTERIOR: STREET IN FRONT OF BUILDING. NIGHT.

VALERIE and a repulsive-looking JANITOR hover in the shadows in the doorway of a building, illuminated sporadically by the head-lights of passing cars. He unlocks the door of the building.

EXTERIOR: ROOFTOP. NIGHT.

The JANITOR leans against a wall. VALERIE is on her knees in front of him.
The camera holds a long close-up on the JANITOR, reminiscent of the Warhol film *Blow Job*. We see the lights of the city behind him.

VALERIE

(*voice-over*)

Prior to the replacement of males by machines, the male should be of use to the female, wait on her, cater to her slightest whim, obey her every command, be totally subservient to her, exist in perfect obedience to her will . . .

Cut to VALERIE asleep on the roof, sometime later. She has made a little nest in one corner: a blanket, a bundle of papers for a pillow, the brown-paper bag with the rest of her possessions.

EXTERIOR: ROOFTOP. EARLY MORNING.

VALERIE stands at the parapet of the rooftop, looking down into the city streets. Dawn is breaking.

Close on VALERIE in profile, looking down on the streets far below. Images of the streets and the cars below, from Valerie's point of view.

MANIFESTO SEQUENCE

> VALERIE
> (*voice-over*)
> Rational men want to be squashed, stepped on, crushed and crunched, treated as the curs, the filth that they are, have their repulsiveness confirmed.

INTERIOR: PUBLIC TOILET. EARLY MORNING.

VALERIE stands at the sink in a public toilet. She is looking in the mirror; we can see the attendant behind her, mopping the floor. VALERIE is very carefully applying makeup: lipstick, eye shadow, a little powder.

MANIFESTO SEQUENCE.

> VALERIE
> (*voice-over*)
> Sick, irrational men will attempt to defend themselves when they see SCUM barreling down on them. Men who are rational, however, won't kick or struggle or

raise a distressing fuss, but will just sit back, relax, enjoy the show, and ride the waves to their demise.

INTERIOR: THE FACTORY. DAY.

VALERIE kicks in the door of the old Factory and stands framed in the entranceway, just as she did the first time she visited. In front of her is a vast, empty silver space, but this time, it really is empty, apart from a couple of packing cases, an overturned chair, the old red couch.

She runs through the Factory, bewildered, panicked. She sees the old mirrored disco ball lying in a corner. She kicks it against a wall and it shatters.

INTERIOR: OLYMPIA PRESS OFFICES. DAY.

A bang as the door slams behind VALERIE.

Tense music as she walks into the offices of Olympia Press, clutch‐ing a brown paper bag.

MARILYN, Girodias's assistant, is at her desk, typing.

VALERIE stands there in silence, watching her.

MARILYN looks up, startled.

> MARILYN
> Oh, Valerie, I didn't see you. What can I do for you?

> VALERIE
> Is Girodias here?

> MARILYN
> (*smiling, apologetic*)
> No, didn't he tell you? He's in Montreal. He won't be back until the weekend.

> VALERIE
> When he comes back, tell him I'm going to kill him.

EXTERIOR: STREET CORNER. SAME AFTERNOON.

VALERIE is leaning against a wall a few yards away from the new Factory entrance.

A cab pulls up, and WARHOL gets out. He is dressed in a brown leather jacket, black T-shirt, pressed black jeans, black Beatle boots.

Simultaneously, DANNY arrives, carrying a bundle of fluorescent tubes. VALERIE joins WARHOL on the sidewalk as he gets out of the cab, and all three enter the building together.

WARHOL

Hi, Valerie. We haven't seen you for a long time.

The same images as before of the floors flashing through the metal grates, but there is no tense music. The three wait in silence, with just the whine of the elevator. WARHOL looks at VALERIE and notices that she is wearing a thick sweater and jacket.

WARHOL

Gee, aren't you hot, Valerie? It's June.

VALERIE doesn't reply to this. She keeps twisting a brown paper bag nervously in her hands.

INTERIOR: THE NEW FACTORY. SAME AFTERNOON.

The new Factory is a very different environment from the old: all polished wood floors, potted plants, mirrors, and art deco desks. FRED HUGHES is at his desk—black glass, identical to Morrissey's—next to an open window overlooking the park, writing a memo. MORRISSEY sits opposite at his desk, talking on the phone to Viva. MARIO AMAYA, an elegant art dealer in a white suit, paces around waiting for WARHOL.

The elevator opens.
WARHOL emerges, followed by VALERIE and DANNY. DANNY disappears into the backrooms.

> WARHOL
>
> Look, Valerie's back. Doesn't she look nice? She's wearing makeup.

> MORRISSEY
> (*sarcastically*)
> Yeah, she looks fabulous. Do you want to talk to Viva?

WARHOL goes up to Morrissey's desk and takes the phone, while MORRISSEY wanders off to the projection room in back.

> FRED
>
> What have you been up to, Valerie—still writing dirty books?

Cut to WARHOL on the phone.
As he talks to Viva on the phone, he stares at his own reflection in the glass-topped desk. Bored, he signals to FRED to take over the conversation.
VALERIE stands there in silence. A very long pause as everyone carries on their activities around her.
She reaches slowly into the paper bag and takes out a .32 automatic pistol. She points it at WARHOL. *Nobody takes any notice.* She raises the gun. WARHOL leans forward to pick up the phone.
VALERIE fires. She misses.

> AMAYA
>
> Hit the floor!

WARHOL drops the phone, jumps up from the desk, looking directly into Valerie's face.

> WARHOL
> No! No! Valerie! Don't do it!

VALERIE fires a second shot. WARHOL falls to the floor, tries to hide under the desk. She moves in, puts the paper bag on the desk. As WARHOL writhes on the floor, she sticks the gun under his arm and fires again. Blood pumps out from his chest, spattering the white telephone cord.

VALERIE crosses over to AMAYA, who is crouching on the ground. Their eyes meet as she stands over him, fires and misses.

AMAYA turns to run. She hits him in the buttock. He staggers up and then falls over, crawling along the floor before staggering up again and crashing through the double doors leading to the backroom.

The fluorescent tubes that Danny had left stacked against the wall slowly topple over and shatter, spraying the floor with broken glass.

FRED is behind his desk, paralyzed with fear, watching VALERIE as she crosses the room to WARHOL's office. She tries to pull the door open.

Cut to GERARD on the other side, desperately holding it shut.

VALERIE gives up on the door.

VALERIE turns and crosses the room to FRED. She stops several feet from him and raises the gun. He begs her not to fire. She aims at his forehead.

> VALERIE
> I have to shoot you.

FRED falls to his knees.

> FRED
> Please don't shoot me, Valerie. You can't. I'm innocent. Please just leave.

Without saying a word, VALERIE backs away to the elevator and presses the button. Then she walks back, aims at Fred's forehead and presses the trigger. The gun jams.
The elevator doors open.

> FRED
> There's the elevator, Valerie. Just take it.

VALERIE runs into it, and the doors close on her.
WARHOL lies on the ground. He looks up and sees hands pulling at him; he sees Billy's face.
The sound of Billy's gasping.

> WARHOL
> (*starts to giggle and then his face creases with pain*)
> Don't laugh. Oh, please don t make me laugh.

BILLY is cradling WARHOL in his lap, like the *Pietà*. Billy's face is contorted with sobs.

EXTERIOR: NEW YORK STREET. EARLY EVENING.

A YOUNG POLICEMAN is standing in the street, directing traffic.
VALERIE approaches him.
She tries to hand him the gun. '

> VALERIE
> You better take this. The police are looking for me
> and want me.

The YOUNG POLICEMAN stares at her in astonishment.

> VALERIE
> I shot Andy Warhol.

(*She opens his hand and makes him take the gun.*)
I had to do it. He had too much control over my
life.

EXTERIOR: WASHINGTON SQUARE PARK. DAY.

Up against the Wall, Motherfucker are performing a street theater action in support of Valerie Solanas before a small hippie
audience. MARK reads this prose poem, which will be accompanied by a classic sixties piece of street theater complete with masks,
mime, etcetera.

> MARK
>
> VALERIE LIVES! . . . Andy Warhol shot by Valerie
> Solanas. Plastic Man versus the Sweet Assassin—the
> face of plastic fascist smashed—the terrorist knows
> where to strike—at the heart—a red plastic inevitable
> exploded—nonman shot by the reality of his dream
> as the cultural assassin emerges—a tough chick with
> a bop cap and a thirty-eight—the true vengeance of
> Dada—tough little chick—the hater of *men* and the
> lover of *man*—with the surgeon's gun—
> *Now*—the Camp Master slain by the Slave—and
> America's white plastic cathedral is ready to burn.
> *Valerie is ours and the Sweet Assassin lives.*
> SCUM in *exile.*

One of the group is painting VALERIE LIVES in big white letters on
a nearby wall.

INTERIOR: ELMHURST HOSPITAL. DAY.

The psychiatrist's report is delivered in voice-over over a series of
hospital scenes, some of them belonging to VALERIE and some to
WARHOL.

PSYCHIATRIST
(*voice-over*)
In regard to the incident on June 3d, the patient says, "I shot Andy Warhol. He is trying to steal all my work." She says that she is "glad that he is in the hospital, and hopes he dies!!" She also complained that "if Andy has really forgiven me, why hasn't he been to see me?"

Close-up of an arm being swabbed with cotton. A threatening-looking hypodermic needle approaches the camera's point of view. The arm flinches. Camera travels up the arm to Valerie's hate-filled eyes as she is given the injection.
Close-up of a fresh white sheet unfolding and tossed onto a bed. Hands tuck hospital corners.
We follow VALERIE as she is led along a corridor, catatonic, her hospital gown flapping open at the back.
The white uniform of a nurse bending over WARHOL and lifting him.
VALERIE in a white, tiled bathroom, naked on a chair, as she is hosed down.
Close on a figure lying under a white sheet. The sheet is lifted. A white hospital gown is gently parted, revealing the raw stitches of Warhol's wounds. A hand carefully begins to clean the wounds.

INTERIOR: CANDY'S ROOM, HOTEL EARLE. DAY.
Close on an image of Candy's hand covering her penis in the mirror.
She tucks it between her legs and observes herself.

CANDY
(*voice-over*)
Dear Stevie,
Everyone's married, and I plan to also. Yes, Pat, I have decided to be sex changed. I am too female to be half-and-half.

CANDY sits back down at her vanity table and resumes writing a letter:

> CANDY
> (*voice-over*)
> There is a very good book on the subject, written by Dr. Harry Benjamin, *The Transsexual Phenomenon*. I think you should read it. Let me know what you think of this step I want to take.

INTERIOR: CHURCH. DAY.

CANDY is in front of a church shrine, her head covered with a black lace scarf. The shrine is surrounded by dozens of candles, dripping wax. CANDY puts ten cents in the collection box, takes a candle, and lights it. Carefully, she takes a small picture of Valerie, clipped from one of the newspaper accounts of the shooting, and places it against the candle.

> CANDY
> (*voice-over*)
> You asked me about writing to Valerie Solanas. I think you should. I know she did a terrible thing, but she has paid or is paying for it, and she needs a friend. It is very thoughtful and kind of you, and you should do it.

CANDY lights another candle and places a small picture of Warhol against it.

CANDY bows her head in prayer.

Caption: AFTER MANY ILLEGAL HORMONE TREATMENTS, CANDY DARLING DIED OF CANCER IN 1975.

INTERIOR: OLYMPIA PRESS OFFICES. DAY.

On the office wall are posters for the *SCUM Manifesto*, and there are piles of the book on the desks and shelves.

Silently, MARILYN hands GIRODIAS a letter. As he opens it, we hear Valerie's voice.

> VALERIE
> (*voice-over*)
>
> Dear Toad,
> Your secret agent knew where I was, because of the transmitter in my uterus. You told him to tell me you don't want me to write you anymore. I know you live for my letters. What else is in your grim, puny life?

Caption: MAURICE GIRODIAS PUBLISHED THE "SCUM MANIFESTO" IN 1968 BUT WENT BANKRUPT SHORTLY AFTERWARDS.
GIRODIAS sighs as he folds the letter and puts it back in its envelope.
Caption: HE RETURNED TO PARIS AND PUBLISHED A BEST-SELLING AUTOBIOGRAPHY BEFORE HE DIED IN 1991.

INTERIOR: MAX'S KANSAS CITY. DAY.

WARHOL, VIVA, and several members of the Factory entourage are having lunch with LAURA. It is a warm September day, and they're sitting in the garden in the back of the restaurant.
A tape recorder is running on the table.
VIVA is in midmonologue:

> VIVA
>
> Andy's shooting was part of a conspiracy against the cultural revolution. Recently, a man leapt over three empty rows in a cinema and punched me as hard as he could. It was during the greenhouse scene of *Amities Particulières,* and I giggled and said, "Gay among the gladioli or faggot among the ferns." It was supposedly a sensitive homosexual film—so tacky.

The others at the table laugh. VIVA carries on regardless.
Camera tracks along the table, through glasses, empty plates, flow-
ers, and Warhol's tape recorder spinning round.

> VIVA
> I was also attacked in my apartment the other night
> by someone whom I had never seen before. It turns
> out he's a professional attacker. All he does is beat
> up people. I really did a job on him. I think I frac-
> tured his skull. I've never seen so much blood.

> WARHOL
> Well, it's our year for crazy people.
> (*Wincing at the memory:*)
> It really is.

> LAURA
> Do you feel all right?

> WARHOL
> Since I was shot, everything is such a dream to me.
> I don't know what anything is about. Like, I don't
> even know whether I'm really alive or—whether I
> died. It's sad. Like I can't say hello or good-bye to
> people. Life is like a dream. What would you call that?

> LAURA
> Are you afraid?

> WARHOL
> That's so funny. I wasn't afraid before. And having
> been dead once, I shouldn't feel fear. But I am afraid.
> I don't understand why. I am afraid of God when
> I'm alone, and I wasn't before. I'm afraid to go to
> the Factory.

WARHOL pulls a false moustache from his pocket and offers it to VIVA, who pastes it over her mouth. He shakes his head. She hands it back to him, and he puts it back in his pocket.

> WARHOL
> (*to* LAURA)
> Are you coming to the party tonight?

EXTERIOR: STUDIO 54. SAME DAY.

Caption: JULY 1977.
At the club entrance, a small crowd dressed in disco regalia— spandex, satin hot pants, halter tops—waits impatiently behind a velvet rope, as a contemptuous DOORMAN inspects it. Through the doorway, we can see darkness, flashing lights, and hear the disco sounds of 1977.

> DOORMAN
> (*bored, examining a list*)
> I don't see your name on the list.

The DOORMAN looks up and respectfully acknowledges a small crowd of celebrities who have arrived, including WARHOL and FRED HUGHES.
A passing car backfires with a bang. WARHOL swivels round and freezes in terror.
Across the street, he sees VALERIE. She is standing quite still, a smile of recognition on her face: it is the same smile she had the night they first met in the Factory.
A van passes between them, blocking her from sight. When it clears, the apparition is gone, and WARHOL is left staring at an empty street.
Caption: ANDY WARHOL NEVER FULLY RECOVERED FROM THE SHOOT- ING. HE DIED AFTER MINOR SURGERY IN NEW YORK HOSPITAL IN 1987.
WARHOL turns round and sees the others staring at him. There is an awkward silence as they turn and walk into the club.

The opening lines of the following manifesto speech float over the ending of this scene.

> VALERIE
> (*voice-over*)
> As for the issue of whether or not to continue to reproduce males, it doesn't follow that, because the male, like disease, has always existed among us that he should continue to exist . . .

MANIFESTO SEQUENCE.

> VALERIE
> Why produce even females? Why should there be future generations? What is their purpose?
> When aging and death are eliminated, why continue to reproduce?

Caption: VALERIE SOLANAS DIED DESTITUTE OF EMPHYSEMA IN SAN FRANCISCO IN 1988.

Fade to black.
As the voice-over ends, the music of the Velvet Underground's "All Tomorrow's Parties" begins and plays over the credits. Credits roll.

SCUM Manifesto

(Society for Cutting up Men)

Valerie Solanas

Life in this society being, at best, an utter bore and no aspect of society being at all relevant to women, there remains to civic-minded, responsible, thrill-seeking females only to overthrow the government, eliminate the money system, institute complete automation and destroy the male sex.

It is now technically possible to reproduce without the aid of males (or, for that matter, females) and to produce only females. We must begin immediately to do so. The male is a biological accident: the y (male) gene is an incomplete x (female) gene, that is, has an incomplete set of chromosomes. In other words, the male is an incomplete female, a walking abortion, aborted at the gene stage. To be male is to be deficient, emotionally limited; maleness is a deficiency disease and males are emotional cripples.

The male is completely egocentric, trapped inside himself, incapable of empathizing or identifying with others, of love, friendship, affection or tenderness. He is a completely isolated unit, incapable of rapport with anyone. His responses are entirely visceral, not cerebral; his intelligence is a mere tool in the service of his drives and needs; he is incapable of mental passion, mental interaction; he can't relate to anything other than his own physical sensations. He is a half dead, unresponsive lump, incapable of giving or receiving pleasure or happiness; consequently, he is at best an utter bore, an inoffensive blob, since only those capable of absorption in others can be charming. He is trapped in a twilight zone halfway between humans and apes, and is far worse off than the apes, because unlike the apes he is capable of a large array of negative feelings—hate, jealousy, contempt, disgust, guilt, shame, doubt—and, moreover he is *aware* of what he is and isn't.

Although completely physical, the male is unfit even for stud service. Even assuming mechanical proficiency, which few men have, he is, first of all, incapable of zestfully, lustfully, tearing off a piece, but is instead eaten up with guilt, shame, fear and insecurity, feelings rooted in male nature, which the most enlightened training can only minimize; second, the physical feeling he attains is next to nothing; and, third, he is not empathizing with his partner, but is obsessed with how he's doing, turning in an A performance, doing a good plumbing job. To call a man an animal is to flatter him; he's a machine, a walking dildo. It's often said that men use women. Use them for what? Surely not pleasure.

Eaten up with guilt, shame, fears and insecurities and obtaining, if he's lucky, a barely perceptible physical feeling, the male is, nonetheless, obsessed with screwing; he'll swim a river of snot, wade nostril-deep through a mile of vomit, if he thinks there'll be a friendly pussy awaiting him. He'll screw a woman he despises, any snaggle-toothed hag, and, furthermore, pay for the opportunity. Why? Relieving physical tension isn't the answer, as masturbation suffices for that. It's not ego satisfaction; that doesn't explain screwing corpses and babies.

Completely egocentric, unable to relate, empathize or identify, and filled with a vast, pervasive, diffuse sexuality, the male is psychically passive. He hates his passivity, so he projects it onto women, defines the male as active, then sets out to prove that he is ("prove he's a Man"). His main means of attempting to prove it is screwing (Big Man with a Big Dick tearing off a Big Piece). Since he's atempting to prove an error, he must "prove" it again and again. Screwing, then, is a desperate, compulsive attempt to prove he's not passive, not a woman; but he *is* passive and *does* want to be a woman.

Being an incomplete female, the male spends his life attempting to complete himself, to become female. He attempts to do this by constantly seeking out, fraternizing with and trying to live through and fuse with the female, and by claiming as his own all female characteristics—emotional strength and independence, forcefulness, dynamism, decisiveness, coolness, objectivity, assertiveness, courage, integrity, vitality, intensity, depth of character, grooviness, etc.—and projecting onto women all male traits—vanity, frivolity, triviality, weakness, etc. It should be said, though, that the male has one glaring area of superiority over the female—public relations. (He has done a brilliant job of convincing millions of women that men are women and women are men.) The male claim that females find fulfillment through motherhood and sexuality reflects what males think they'd find fulfilling if they were female.

Women, in other words, don't have penis envy; men have pussy envy. When the male accepts his passivity, defines himself as a woman (Males as well as females think men are women and women are men), and becomes a transvestite he loses his desire to screw (or to do anything else, for that matter; he fulfills himself as a drag queen) and gets his cock chopped off. He then achieves a continuous diffuse sexual feeling from "being a woman." Screwing is, for a man, a defense against his desire to be female. Sex is itself a sublimation.

The male, because of his obsession to compensate for not being female combined with his inability to relate and to feel compassion, has made of the world a shitpile. He is responsible for:

WAR: The male's normal method of compensation for not being female, namely, getting his Big Gun off, is grossly inadequate, as he can get it off only a very limited number of times; so he gets it off on a really massive scale, and proves to the entire world that he's a "Man." Since he has no compassion or ability to empathize or identify, proving his manhood is worth an endless number of lives, including his own—his own life being worthless, he would rather go out in a blaze of glory than plod grimly on for fifty more years.

NICENESS, POLITENESS AND "DIGNITY": Every man, deep down, knows he's a worthless piece of shit. Overwhelmed by a sense of animalism and deeply ashamed of it; wanting, not to express himself, but to hide from others his total physicality, total egocentricity, the hate and contempt he feels for other men, and to hide from himself the hate and contempt he suspects other men feel for him; having a crudely constructed nervous system that is easily upset by the least display of emotion or feeling, the male tries to enforce a "social" code that ensures a perfect blandness, unsullied by the slightest trace of feeling or upsetting opinion. He uses terms like "copulate," "sexual congress," "have relations with" (To men "*sexual* relations" is a redundancy), overlaid with stilted manners; the suit on the chimp.

MONEY, MARRIAGE AND PROSTITUTION, WORK AND PREVENTION OF AN AUTOMATED SOCIETY: There is no human reason for money or for anyone to work. All non-creative jobs (practically all jobs now being done) could have been automated long ago, and in a moneyless society everyone can have as much of the best of everything as she wants. But there are non-human, male reasons for maintaining the money-work system:

1. Pussy. Despising his highly inadequate self, overcome with intense anxiety and a deep, profound loneliness when by his empty self, despite to attach himself to any female in dim hopes of completing himself, in the mystical belief that by touching gold he'll turn to gold, the male craves the continuous companionship of women. The company of the lowest female is preferable to his own or that of other men, who serve only to remind him of his repulsiveness. But females, unless very young or very sick, must be coerced or bribed into male company.

2. Supply the non-relating male with the delusion of usefulness, and enable him to try to justify his existence by digging holes and filling them up. Leisure time horrifies the male, who will have nothing to do but contemplate his grotesque self. Unable to relate or to love, the male must work. Females crave

absorbing, emotionally satisfying, meaningful activity, but lacking the opportunity or ability for this, they prefer to idle and waste away their time in ways of their own choosing—sleeping, shopping, bowling, shooting pool, playing cards and other games, breeding, reading, walking around, daydreaming, eating, playing with themselves, popping pills, going to the movies, getting analyzed, traveling, raising dogs and cats, lolling on the beach, swimming, watching T.V., listening to music, decorating their houses, gardening, sewing, nightclubbing, dancing, visiting, "improving their minds" (taking courses), and absorbing "culture" (lectures, plays, concerts, "arty" movies). Therefore, many females would, even assuming complete economic equality between the sexes, prefer living with males or peddling their asses on the street, thus having most of their time for themselves, to spending many hours of their days doing boring, stultifying non-creative work for somebody else, functioning as less than animals, as machines, or, at best—if able to get a "good" job—co-managing the shitpile. What will liberate women, therefore, from male control is the total elimination of the money-work system, not the attainment of economic equality with men within it.

3. Power and control. Unmasterful in his personal relations with women, the male attains to general masterfulness by the manipulation of money and of everything and everybody controlled by money, in other words, of everything and everybody.

4. Love substitute. Unable to give love or affection, the male gives money. It makes him feel motherly. The mother gives milk; he gives bread. He is the Breadwinner.

5. Provides the male with a goal. Incapable of enjoying the moment, the male needs something to look forward to, and money provides him with an eternal, never-ending goal: Just think what you could do with 80 trillion dollars—Invest it! And in three years time you'd have 300 trillion dollars!!!

6. Provides the basis for the male's major opportunity to control and manipulate—fatherhood.

FATHERHOOD AND MENTAL ILLNESS (fear, cowardice, timidity, humility, insecurity, passivity): Mother wants what's best for her kids; Daddy only wants what's best for Daddy, that is peace and quiet, pandering to his delusion of dignity ("respect"), a good reflection on himself (status) and the opportunity to control and manipulate, or, if he's an "enlightened" father, to "give guidance." His daughter, in addition, he wants sexually— He gives her *hand* in marriage; the other part is for him. Daddy, unlike Mother, can never give in to his kids, as he must, at all costs, preserve his delusion of decisiveness, forcefulness, always-rightness and strength. Never getting one's way leads to lack of self-confidence in one's ability to cope with the world and to a passive acceptance of the status quo. Mother loves her kids, although she sometimes gets angry, but anger blows over quickly and even while it exists, doesn't preclude love and basic acceptance. Emotionally diseased Daddy doesn't love his kids; he approves of them—if they're "good," that is, if they're nice, "respectful," obedient, subservient to his will, quiet and not given to unseemly displays of temper that would be most upsetting to Daddy's easily disturbed male nervous system—in other words, if they're passive vegetables. If they're not "good," he doesn't get angry—not if he's a modern, "civilized" father (The old-fashioned ranting, raving brute is preferable, as he is so ridiculous he can be easily despised)—but rather expresses disapproval, a state that, unlike anger, endures and precludes a basic acceptance, leaving the kid with a feeling of worthlessness and a lifelong obsession with being approved of; the result is fear of independent thought, as this leads to unconventional, disapproved of opinions and way of life.

For the kid to want Daddy's approval it must respect Daddy, and, being garbage, Daddy can make sure that he is respected only by remaining aloof, by distantness, by acting on the precept "familiarity breeds contempt," which is, of course, true, if one is contemptible. By being distant and aloof, he is able to remain unknown, mysterious, and, thereby, to inspire fear ("respect").

Disapproval of emotional "scenes" leads to fear of strong emotion, fear of one's own anger and hatred, and to a fear of facing reality, as facing it leads at first to anger and hatred. Fear of anger and hatred combined with a lack of self-confidence in one's ability to cope with and change the world, or even to affect in the slightest way one's own destiny, leads to a mindless belief that the world and most people in it are nice and that the most banal, trivial amusements are great fun and deeply pleasurable.

The effect of fatherhood on males, specifically, is to make them "Men," that is, highly defensive of all impulses to passivity, faggotry, and of desires to be female. Every boy wants to imitate his mother, be her, fuse with her, but Daddy forbids this; *he* is the mother; *he* gets to fuse with her. So he tells the boy, sometimes directly, sometimes indirectly, to not be a sissy, to act like a "Man." The boy, scared shitless of and "respecting" his father, complies, and becomes just like Daddy, that model of "Man"-hood, the all American ideal—the well-behaved heterosexual dullard.

The effect of fatherhood on females is to make them male—dependent, passive, domestic, animalistic, nice, insecure, approval and security seekers, cowardly, humble, "respectful" of authorities and men, closed, not fully responsive, half dead, trivial, dull, conventional, flattened out and thoroughly contemptible. Daddy's Girl, always tense and fearful, uncool, unanalytical, lacking objectivity, appraises Daddy, and thereafter, other men, against a background of fear ("respect") and is not only unable to see the empty shell behind the aloof facade, but accepts the male definition of himself as superior, as a female, and of herself, as inferior, as a male, which, thanks to Daddy, she really is.

It is the increase of fatherhood, resulting from the increased and more widespread affluence that fatherhood needs in order to thrive, that has caused the general increase of mindlessness and the decline of women in the U.S. since the 1920's. The close association of affluence with fatherhood has led, for the most part, to only the wrong girls, namely, the "privileged," middle-class girls, getting "educated."

The effect of fathers, in sum, has been to corrode the world with maleness. The male has a negative Midas Touch—everything he touches turns to shit.

SUPPRESSION OF INDIVIDUALITY, ANIMALISM (domesticity and motherhood) AND FUNCTIONALISM: The male is just a bundle of conditioned reflexes, incapable of a mentally free response; he is tied to his early conditioning, determined completely by his past experiences. His earliest experiences are with his mother, and he is throughout his life tied to her. It never becomes completely clear to the male that he is not part of his mother, that he is he and she is she.

His greatest need is to be guided, sheltered, protected and admired by Mama (Men expect women to adore what men shrink from in horror—themselves), and, being completely physical, he yearns to spend his time (that's not spent "out in the world" grimly defending against his passivity) wallowing in basic animal activities—eating, sleeping, shitting, relaxing and being soothed by Mama. Passive, rattle-headed Daddy's Girl, ever eager for approval, for a pat on the head, for the "respect" of any passing piece of garbage, is easily reduced to Mama, mindless ministrator to physical needs, soother of the weary, apey brow, booster of the puny ego, appreciator of the contemptible, a hot water bottle with tits.

The reduction to animals of the women of the most backward segment of society—the "privileged, educated" middle class, the backwash of humanity—where Daddy reigns supreme, has been so thorough that they try to groove on labor pains and lie around in the most advanced nation in the world in the middle of the twentieth century with babies chomping away on their tits. It's not for the kids' sake, though, that the "experts" tell women that Mama should stay home and grovel in animalism, but for Daddy's; the tit's for Daddy to hang onto; the labor pains for Daddy to vicariously groove on (Half dead, he needs awfully strong stimuli to make him respond).

Reducing the female to an animal, to Mama, to a male, is necessary for psychological as well as practical reasons: the male is a mere member of the species, interchangeable with every other male. He has no deep-seated individuality, which stems from what intrigues you, what outside yourself absorbs you, what you're in relation to. Completely self-absorbed, capable of being in relation only to their bodies and physical sensations, males differ from each other only to the degree and in the ways they attempt to defend against their passivity and against their desire to be female.

The female's individuality, which he is acutely aware of, but which he doesn't comprehend and isn't capable of relating to or grasping emotionally, frightens and upsets him and fills him with envy. So he denies it in her and proceeds to define everyone in terms of his or her function or use, assigning to himself, of course, the most important functions—doctor, president, scientist— thereby providing himself with an identity, if not individuality, and tries to convince himself and women (he's succeeded best at convincing women) that the female function is to bear and raise children and to relax, comfort and boost the ego of the male; that her function is such as to make her interchangeable with every other female. In actual fact, the female function is to relate, groove, love and be herself, irreplaceable by anyone else; the male function is to produce sperm. We now have sperm banks.

PREVENTION OF PRIVACY: Although the male, being ashamed of what he is and of almost everything he does, insists on privacy and secrecy in all aspects of his life, he has no real regard for privacy. Being empty, not being a complete, separate being, having no self to groove on and needing to be constantly in female company, he sees nothing at all wrong in intruding himself on any woman's thoughts, even a total stranger's, anywhere at any time, but rather feels indignant and insulted when put down for doing so, as well as confused—he can't, for the life of him, understand why anyone would prefer so much as one minute of solitude to the company of any creep around. Wanting to become a woman, he strives to be constantly around females, which is the closest he can get to becoming one, so he created a "society" based on the family—a male-female couple and their kids (the excuse for the family's existence), who live virtually on top of one another, un-scrupulously violating the females' rights, privacy and sanity.

ISOLATION, SUBURBS AND PREVENTION OF COMMUNITY:
Our society is not a community, but merely a collection of iso-lated family units. Desperately insecure, fearing his woman will leave him if she is exposed to other men or to anything remotely resembling life, the male seeks to isolate her from other men and from what little civilization there is, so he moves her out to the suburbs, a collection of self-absorbed couples and their kids. Iso-lation enables him to try to maintain his pretense of being an individual by becoming a "rugged individualist," a loner, equat-ing non-cooperation and solitariness with individuality.

There is yet another reason for the male to isolate himself: every man is an island. Trapped inside himself, emotionally iso-lated, unable to relate, the male has a horror of civilization, people, cities, situations requiring an ability to understand and relate to people. So, like a scared rabbit, he scurries off, dragging Daddy's little asshole along with him to the wilderness, the suburbs, or, in the case of the "hippy"—he's way out, Man!—all the way out to the cow pasture where he can fuck and breed undisturbed and mess around with his beads and flute.

The "hippy," whose desire to be a "Man," a "rugged in-dividualist," isn't quite as strong as the average man's, and who, in addition, is excited by the thought of having lots of women accessible to him, rebels against the harshness of a Breadwinner's life and the monotony of one woman. In the name of sharing and cooperation, he forms the commune or tribe, which, for all its togetherness and partly because of it (the commune, being an extended family, is an extended violation of the females' rights, privacy and sanity) is no more a community than normal "society."

A true community consists of individuals—not mere species members, not couples—respecting each other's individuality and privacy, at the same time interacting with each other mentally and emotionally—free spirits in free relation to each other— and cooperating with each other to achieve common ends. Traditionalists say the basic unit of "society" is the family; "hippies" say the tribe; no one says the individual.

The "hippy" babbles on about individuality, but has no more conception of it than any other man. He desires to get back to Nature, back to the wilderness, back to the home of the furry animals that he's not one of, away from the city, where there is at least a trace, a bare beginning of civilization, to live at the species level, his time taken up with simple, non-intellectual activities— farming, fucking, bead stringing. The most important activity of the commune, the one on which it is based, is gang-banging. The "hippy" is enticed to the commune mainly by the prospect of all the free pussy—the main commodity to be shared, to be had just for the asking, but, blinded by greed, he fails to anticipate all the other men he has to share with, or the jealousies and possessiveness of the pussies themselves.

Men cannot cooperate to achieve a common end, because each man's end is all the pussy for himself. The commune, therefore, is doomed to failure: each "hippy" will, in panic, grab the first simpleton who digs him and whisk her off to the suburbs as fast as he can. The male cannot progress socially, but merely swings back and forth from isolation to gang-banging.

CONFORMITY: Although he wants to be an individual, the male is scared of anything about him that is the slightest bit different from other men; it causes him to suspect he's not really a "Man," that he's passive and totally sexual, a highly upsetting suspicion. If other men are A and he's not, he must not be a man; he must be a fag. So he tries to affirm his "Manhood" by being like all the other men. Differentness in other men, as well as in himself, threatens him; it means *they're* fags whom he must at all costs avoid, so he tries to make sure that all other men conform.

The male dares to be different to the degree that he accepts his passivity and his desire to be female, his fagginess. The farthest out male is the drag queen, but he, although different from most men, is exactly like all other drag queens; like the functionalist, he has an identity—he is a female. He tries to define all his troubles away—but still no individuality. Not completely convinced that he's a woman, highly insecure about being sufficiently female, he conforms compulsively to the man-made feminine stereotype, ending up as nothing but a bundle of stilted mannerisms.

To be sure he's a "Man," the male must see to it that the female be clearly a "Woman," the opposite of a "Man," that is; the female must act like a faggot. And Daddy's Girl, all of whose female instincts were wrenched out of her when little, easily and obligingly adapts herself to the role.

AUTHORITY AND GOVERNMENT: Having no sense of right or wrong, no conscience, which can only stem from an ability to empathize with others . . . having no faith in his non-existent self, being necessarily competitive and, by nature, unable to cooperate, the male feels a need for external guidance and control. So he created authorities—priests, experts, bosses, leaders, etc.—and government. Wanting the female (Mama) to guide him, but unable to accept this fact (He is, after all, a *MAN*), wanting to play Woman, to usurp her function as Guider and Protector, he sees to it that all authorities are male.

There's no reason why a society consisting of rational beings capable of empathizing with each other, complete and having no natural reason to compete, should have a government, laws or leaders.

PHILOSOPHY, RELIGION AND MORALITY BASED ON SEX: The male's inability to relate to anybody or anything makes his life pointless and meaningless (The ultimate male insight is that life is absurd), so he invented philosophy and religion. Being empty, he looks outward, not only for guidance and control, but for salvation and for the meaning of life. Happiness being for him impossible on this earth, he invented Heaven.

For a man, having no ability to empathize with others and being totally sexual, "wrong" is sexual "license" and engaging in "deviant" ("unmanly") sexual practices that is, not defending against his passivity and total sexuality which, if indulged, would destroy "civilization," since "civilization" is based entirely on the male need to defend himself against these characteristics. For a woman (according to men) "wrong" is any behavior that would entice men into sexual "license"—that is, not placing male needs above her own and not being a faggot.

Religion not only provides the male with a goal (Heaven) and helps keep women tied to men, but offers rituals through which he can try to expiate the guilt and shame he feels at not defending himself enough against his sexual impulses; in essence, that guilt and shame he feels at being a male.

Most men, utterly cowardly, project their inherent weaknesses onto women, label them female weaknesses and believe themselves to have female strengths; most philosophers, not quite so cowardly, face the fact that male lacks exist in men, but still can't face the fact that they exist in men only. So they label the male condition the Human Condition, pose their nothingness problem, which horrifies them, as a philosophical dilemma, thereby giving stature to their animalism, grandiloquently label their nothingness their "Identity Problem," and proceed to prattle on pompously about the "Crisis of the Individual," the "Essence of Being," "Existence Preceding Essence," "Existential Modes of Being," etc., etc.

A woman not only takes her identity and individuality for granted, but knows instinctively that the only wrong is to hurt others, and that the meaning of life is love.

PREJUDICE (racial, ethnic, religious, etc.): The male needs scapegoats onto whom he can project his failings and inadequacies and upon whom he can vent his frustration at not being female.

COMPETITION, PRESTIGE, STATUS, FORMAL EDUCATION, IGNORANCE AND SOCIAL AND ECONOMIC CLASSES: Having an obsessive desire to be admired by women, but no intrinsic worth, the male constructs a highly artificial society enabling him to appropriate the appearance of worth through money, prestige, "high" social class, degrees, professional position and knowledge, and by pushing as many other men as possible down professionally, socially, economically, and educationally.

The purpose of "higher" education is not to educate but to exclude as many as possible from the various professions.

The male, although able to understand and use knowledge and ideas, is unable to relate to them, to grasp them emotionally; he does not value knowledge and ideas for their own sake (they're just means to ends) and, consequently, feels no need for mental companions, no need to cultivate the intellectual potentialities of others. On the contrary, the male has a vested interest in ignorance; he knows that an enlightened, aware female population will mean the end of him. The healthy, conceited female wants the company of equals whom she can respect and groove on; the male and the sick, insecure, unself-confident male female crave the company of worms.

No genuine social revolution can be accomplished by the male, as the male on top wants the status quo, and all the male on the bottom wants is to be the male on top. The male "rebel" is a farce; this is the male's "society," made by *him* to satisfy *his* needs. He's never satisfied, because he's not capable of being satisfied. Ultimately, what the male "rebel" is rebelling against is being male. The male changes only when forced to do so by technology, when he has no choice, when "society" reaches the stage where he must change or die. We're at that stage now; if women don't get their asses in gear fast, we may very well all die.

PREVENTION OF CONVERSATION: Being completely self-centered and unable to relate to anything outside himself, the male's "conversation," when not about himself, is an impersonal droning on, removed from anything of human value. Male "intellectual conversation" is a strained, compulsive attempt to impress the female.

Daddy's Girl, passive, adaptable, respectful of and in awe of the male, allows him to impose his hideously dull chatter on her. This is not too difficult for her, as the tension and anxiety, the lack of cool, the insecurity and self-doubt, the unsureness of her own feelings and sensations that Daddy instilled in her make her perceptions superficial and render her unable to see that the male's babble is a babble; like the aesthete "appreciating" the blob that's labeled "Great Art," she believes she's grooving on what bores the shit out of her. Not only does she permit his babble to dominate, she adapts her own "conversation" accordingly.

Trained from early childhood in niceness, politeness and "dignity," in pandering to the male need to disguise his animalism, she obligingly reduces her "conversation" to small talk, a bland, insipid avoidance of any topic beyond the utterly trivial—or, if "educated," to "intellectual" discussion, that is, impersonal discoursing on irrelevant abstractions—the Gross National Product, the Common Market, the influence of Rimbaud on symbolist painting. So adept is she at pandering that it eventually becomes second nature and she continues to pander to men even when in the company of other females only.

Apart from pandering, her "conversation" is further limited by her insecurity about expressing deviant, original opinions and the self-absorption based on insecurity and that prevents her conversation from being charming. Niceness, politeness, "dignity," insecurity and self-absorption are hardly conducive to intensity and wit, qualities a conversation must have to be worthy of the name. Such conversation is hardly rampant, as only completely self-confident, arrogant, outgoing, proud, tough-minded females are capable of intense, bitchy, witty conversation.

PREVENTION OF FRIENDSHIP AND LOVE: Men have contempt for themselves, for all other men and for all women who respect and pander to them; the insecure, approval-seeking, pandering male females have contempt for themselves and for all

women like them; the self-confident, swinging, thrill-seeking female females have contempt for men and for the pandering male
females. In short, contempt is the order of the day.

Love is not dependency or sex, but friendship, and, therefore, love can't exist between two males, between a male and a
female or between two females, one or both of whom is a mindless, insecure, pandering male; like conversation, love can exist
only between two secure, free-wheeling, independent, groovy
female females, since friendship is based on respect, not contempt.

Even among groovy females deep friendships seldom occur in adulthood, as almost all of them are either tied up with
men in order to survive economically, or bogged down in hack-
ing their way through the jungle and in trying to keep their heads
above the amorphous mass. Love can't flourish in a society based
on money and meaningless work; it requires complete economic
as well as personal freedom, leisure time and the opportunity to
engage in intensely absorbing, emotionally satisfying activities
which, when shared with those you respect, lead to deep friendship. Our "society" provides practically no opportunity to engage
in such activities.

Having stripped the world of conversation, friendship and
love, the male offers us these paltry substitutes:

"GREAT ART" AND "CULTURE": The male "artist" attempts
to solve his dilemma of not being able to live, of not being female,
by constructing a highly artificial world in which the male is
heroized, that is, displays female traits, and the female is reduced
to highly limited, insipid subordinate roles that is, to being male.

The male "artistic" aim being, not to communicate (having nothing inside him, he has nothing to say), but to disguise
his animalism, he resorts to symbolism and obscurity ("deep"
stuff). The vast majority of people, particularly the "educated"
ones, lacking faith in their own judgment, humble, respectful of
authority ("Daddy knows best" is translated into adult language
as "Critic knows best," "Writer knows best," "Ph.D. knows

best"), are easily conned into believing that obscurity, evasiveness, incomprehensibility, indirectness, ambiguity and boredom are marks of depth and brilliance.

"Great Art" proves that men are superior to women, that men are women, being labeled "Great Art," almost all of which, as the anti-feminists are fond of reminding us, was created by men. We know that "Great Art" is great because male authorities have told us so, and we can't claim otherwise, as only those with exquisite sensitivities far superior to ours can perceive and appreciate the greatness, the proof of their superior sensitivity being that they appreciate the slop that they appreciate.

Appreciating is the sole diversion of the "cultivated"; passive and incompetent, lacking imagination and wit, they must try to make do with that; unable to create their own diversions, to create a little world of their own, to affect in the smallest way their environments, they must accept what's given; unable to create or relate, they spectate. Absorbing "culture" is a desperate, frantic attempt to groove in an ungroovy world, to escape the horror of a sterile, mindless existence. "Culture" provides a sop to the egos of the incompetent, a means of rationalizing passive spectating; they can pride themselves on their ability to appreciate the "finer" things, to see a jewel where there is only a turd (they want to be admired for admiring). Lacking faith in their ability to change anything, resigned to the status quo, they *have* to see beauty in turds, because, so far as they can see, turds are all they'll ever have.

The veneration of "Art" and "Culture"—besides leading many women into boring, passive activity that distracts from more important and rewarding activities, and from cultivating active abilities—allows the "artist" to be set up as one possessing superior feelings, perceptions, insights and judgments, thereby undermining the faith of insecure women in the value and validity of their own feelings, perceptions, insights and judgments.

The male, having a very limited range of feelings and, consequently, very limited perceptions, insights and judgments, needs the "artist" to guide him, to tell him what life is all about. But the male "artist," being totally sexual, unable to relate to anything beyond his own physical sensations, having nothing to express beyond the insight that for the male life is meaningless and absurd, cannot be an artist. How can he who is not capable of life tell us what life is all about? A "male artist" is a contradiction in terms. A degenerate can only produce degenerate "art." The true artist is every self-confident, healthy female, and in a female society the only Art, the only Culture, will be conceited, kookie, funky females grooving on each other and on everything else in the universe.

SEXUALITY: Sex is not part of a relationship; on the contrary, it is a solitary experience, non-creative, a gross waste of time. The female can easily—far more easily than she may think—condition away her sex drive, leaving her completely cool and cerebral and free to pursue truly worthy relationships and activities; but the male, who seems to dig women sexually and who seeks constantly to arouse them, stimulates the highly sexed female to frenzies of lust, throwing her into a sex bag from which few women ever escape. The lecherous male excites the lustful female; he *has* to—when the female transcends her body, rises above animalism, the male, whose ego consists of his cock, will disappear.

Sex is the refuge of the mindless. And the more mindless the woman, the more deeply embedded in the male "culture," in short, the nicer she is, the more sexual she is. The nicest women in our "society" are raving sex maniacs. But, being just awfully, awfully nice they don't, of course, descend to fucking—that's uncouth—rather they make love, commune by means of their bodies and establish sensual rapport; the literary ones are attuned to the throb of Eros and attain a clutch upon the Universe; the religious have spiritual communion with the Divine Sensualism; the mystics merge with the Erotic Principle and blend with the Cosmos, and the acid heads contact their erotic cells.

On the other hand, those females least embedded in the male "culture," the least nice, those crass and simple souls who reduce fucking to fucking, who are too childish for the grown-up world of suburbs, mortgages, mops and baby shit, too selfish to raise kids and husbands, too uncivilized to give a shit for anyone's opinion of them, too arrogant to respect Daddy, the "Greats" or the deep wisdom of the Ancients, who trust only their own animal, gutter instincts, who equate Culture with chicks, whose sole diversion is prowling for emotional thrills and excitement, who are given to disgusting, nasty, upsetting "scenes," hateful, violent bitches given to slamming those who unduly irritate them in the teeth, who'd sink a shiv into a man's chest or ram an ice pick up his asshole as soon as look at him, if they knew they could get away with it, in short, those who, by the standards of our "culture," are SCUM . . . these females are cool and relatively cerebral and skirting asexuality.

Unhampered by propriety, niceness, discretion, public opinion, "morals," the "respect" of assholes, always funky, dirty, low-down, SCUM gets around . . . and around and around . . . they've seen the whole show—every bit of it—the fucking scene, the sucking scene, the dick scene, the dike scene—they've covered the whole waterfront, been under every dock and pier—the peter pier, the pussy pier . . . you've got to go through a lot of sex to get to anti-sex, and SCUM's been through it all, and they're now ready for a new show; they want to crawl out from under the dock, move, take off, sink out. But SCUM doesn't yet prevail; SCUM's still in the gutter of our "society," which, if it's not deflected from it's present course and if the Bomb doesn't drop on it, will hump itself to death.

BOREDOM: Life in a "society" made by and for creatures who, when they are not grim and depressing, are utter bores, can only be, when not grim and depressing, an utter bore.

SECRECY, CENSORSHIP, SUPPRESSION OF KNOWLEDGE AND IDEAS, AND EXPOSÉS: Every male's deep-seated, secret, most hideous fear is the fear of being discovered to be not a female, but a male, a subhuman animal. Although niceness, politeness and "dignity" suffice to prevent his exposure on a personal level, in order to prevent the general exposure of the male sex as a whole and to maintain his unnatural dominant position in "society," the male must resort to:

1. Censorship. Responding reflexly to isolated words and phrases rather than cerebrally to overall meanings, the male attempts to prevent the arousal and discovery of his animalism by censoring not only "pornography," but any work containing "dirty" words, no matter in what context they are used.

2. Suppression of all ideas and knowledge that might expose him or threaten his dominant position in "society." Much biological and psychological data is suppressed, because it is proof of the male's gross inferiority to the female. Also, the problem of mental illness will never be solved while the male maintains control, because first, men have a vested interest in it—only females who have very few of their marbles will allow males the slightest bit of control over anything, and second, the male cannot admit to the role that fatherhood plays in causing mental illness.

3. Exposés. The male's chief delight in life—insofar as the tense, grim male can ever be said to delight in anything—is in exposing others. It doesn't much matter what they're exposed as, so long as they're exposed; it distracts attention from himself. Exposing others as enemy agents (Communists and Socialists) is one of his favorite pastimes, as it removes the source of the threat to him not only from himself, but from the country and the Western world. The bugs up his ass aren't in him; they're in Russia.

DISTRUST: Unable to empathize or feel affection or loyalty, being exclusively out for himself, the male has no sense of fair play; cowardly, needing constantly to pander to the female to win her approval, always on edge lest his animalism, his maleness be discovered, always needing to cover up, he must lie constantly; being empty, he has no honor or integrity—he doesn't know what those words mean. The male, in short, is treacherous, and the only appropriate attitude in a male "society" is cynicism and distrust.

UGLINESS: Being totally sexual, incapable of cerebral or aesthetic responses, totally materialistic and greedy, the male, besides inflicting on the world "Great Art," has decorated his unlandscaped cities with ugly buildings (both inside and out), ugly decors, billboards, highways, cars, garbage trucks and, most notably, his own putrid self.

HATE AND VIOLENCE: The male is eaten up with tension, with frustration at not being female, at not being capable of ever achieving satisfaction or pleasure of any kind; eaten up with hate, not rational hate that is directed at those who abuse or insult you, but irrational, indiscriminate hate . . . hatred, at bottom, of his own worthless self.

Violence serves as an outlet for his hate and, in addition, the male being capable only of sexual responses and needing very strong stimuli to stimulate his half-dead self, provides him with a little sexual thrill.

DISEASE AND DEATH: All diseases are curable, and the aging process and death are due to disease; it is possible, therefore, never to age and to live forever. In fact, the problems of aging and death could be solved within a few years, if an all-out, massive scientific assault were made on the problem. This, however, will not occur within the male establishment, because:

1. The many male scientists who shy away from biological research, terrified of the discovery that males are females, and show marked preference for virile, "manly" war and death programs.

2. The discouragement of many potential scientists from scientific careers by the rigidity, boringness, expensiveness, time-consumingness and unfair exclusivity of our "higher" educational system.

3. Propaganda disseminated by insecure male professionals, who jealously guard their positions, that only a highly select few can comprehend abstract scientific concepts.

4. Widespread lack of self-confidence brought about by the father system that discourages many talented girls from becoming scientists.

5. Lack of automation. There now exists a wealth of data which, if sorted out and correlated, would reveal the cure for cancer and several other diseases and possibly the key to life itself. But the data is so massive it requires high speed computers to correlate it all. The institution of computers will be delayed interminably under the male control system, since the male has a horror of being replaced by machines.

6. The money system. Most of the few scientists around who aren't working on death programs are tied up doing research for corporations.

7. The male likes death—it excites him sexually and, already dead inside, he wants to die.

Incapable of a positive state of happiness, which is the only thing that can justify one's existence, the male is, at best, relaxed, comfortable, neutral, and this condition is extremely short-lived, as boredom, a negative state, soon sets in; he is, therefore, doomed to an existence of suffering relieved only by occasional, fleeting stretches of restfulness, which state he can achieve only at the expense of some female. The male is, by his very nature, a leech, an emotional parasite and therefore, not ethically entitled to live, as no one has the right to live at someone else's expense.

Just as humans have a prior right to existence over dogs by virtue, of being more highly evolved and having a superior consciousness, so women have a prior right to existence over men. The elimination of any male is, therefore, a righteous and good act, an act highly beneficial to women as well as an act of mercy.

However, this moral issue will eventually be rendered academic by the fact that the male is gradually eliminating himself. In addition to engaging in the time-honored and classical wars and race riots, men are more and more either becoming fags or are obliterating themselves through drugs. The female, whether she likes it or not, will eventually take complete charge, if for no other reason than that she will have to—the male, for practical purposes, won't exist.

Accelerating this trend is the fact that more and more males are acquiring enlightened self-interest; they're realizing more and more that the female interest is their interest, that they can live only through the female and that the more the female is encouraged to live, to fulfill herself, to be a female and not a male, the more nearly *he* lives; he's coming to see that it's easier and more satisfactory to live *through* her than to try to *become* her and usurp her qualities, claim them as his own, push the female down and claim she's a male. The fag, who accepts his maleness, that is, his passivity and total sexuality, his femininity, is also best served by women being truly female, as it would then be easier for him to be male, feminine. If men were wise they would seek to become really female, would do intensive biological research that would lead to men, by means of operations on the brain and nervous system, being able to be transformed in psyche, as well as body, into women.

Whether to continue to use females for reproduction or to reproduce in the laboratory will also become academic: what will happen when every female, twelve and over, is routinely taking the Pill and there are no longer any accidents? How many women will deliberately allow themselves to get pregnant? No, Virginia, women don't just adore being brood mares, despite what the mass of robot, brainwashed women will say. Should a certain percentage of women be set aside by force to serve as brood mares for the species? Obviously, this will not do. The answer is laboratory reproduction of babies.

As for the issue of whether or not to continue to reproduce males, it doesn't follow that because the male, like disease, has always existed among us that he should continue to exist. When genetic control is possible—and it soon will be—it goes without saying that we should produce only whole, complete beings, not physical defects or deficiencies, including emotional deficiencies, such as maleness. Just as the deliberate production of blind people would be highly immoral, so would be the deliberate production of emotional cripples.

Why produce even females? Why should there be future generations? What is their purpose? When aging and death are eliminated, why continue to reproduce? Even if they are not eliminated, why reproduce? Why should we care what happens when we're dead? Why should we care that there is no younger generation to succeed us?

Eventually the natural course of events, of social evolution, will lead to total female control of the world and, subsequently, to the cessation of the production of males and, ultimately, to the cessation of the production of females.

But SCUM is impatient; SCUM is not consoled by the thought that future generations will thrive; SCUM wants to grab some swinging living for itself. And, if a large majority of women were SCUM, they could acquire complete control of this country within a few weeks simply by withdrawing from the labor force, thereby paralyzing the entire nation. Additional measures, any one of which would be sufficient to completely disrupt the economy and everything else, would be for women to declare themselves off the money system, stop buying, just loot and simply refuse to obey all laws they don't care to obey. The police force, National Guard, Army, Navy and Marines combined couldn't squelch a rebellion of over half the population, particularly when it's made up of people they are utterly helpless without.

If all women simply left men, refused to have anything to do with any of them, ever, all men, the government and the national economy would collapse completely. Even without leaving men, women who are aware of the extent of their superiority to and power over men, could acquire complete control over everything within a few weeks, could effect a total submission of males to females. In a sane society the male would trot along obediently after the female. The male is docile and easily led, easily subjected to the domination of any female who cares to domi-

nate him. The male, in fact, wants desperately to be led by females, wants Mama in charge, wants to abandon himself to her
care. But this is not a sane society, and most women are not even
dimly aware of where they're at in relation to men.

The conflict, therefore, is not between females and males,
but between SCUM—dominant, secure, self-confident, nasty,
violent, selfish, independent, proud, thrill-seeking, freewheeling
arrogant females, who consider themselves fit to rule the universe,
who have free-wheeled to the limits of this "society" and are ready
to wheel on to something far beyond what it has to offer—and
nice, passive, accepting, "cultivated," polite, dignified, subdued,
dependent, scared, mindless, insecure, approval-seeking Daddy's
Girls, who can't cope with the unknown, who want to continue
to wallow in the sewer that is, at least, familiar, who want to hang
back with the apes, who feel secure only with Big Daddy standing by, with a big, strong man to lean on and with a fat, hairy
face in the White House, who are too cowardly to face up to the
hideous reality of what a man is, what Daddy is, who have cast
their lot with the swine, who have adapted themselves to animalism, feel superficially comfortable with it and know no other way
of "life," who have reduced their minds, thoughts and sights
to the male level, who, lacking sense, imagination and wit can
have value only in a male "society," who can have a place in the
sun, or, rather, in the slime, only as soothers, ego boosters, relax-
ers and breeders, who are dismissed as inconsequents by other
females, who project their deficiencies, their maleness, onto all
females and see the female as a worm.

But SCUM is too impatient to hope and wait for the
debrainwashing of millions of assholes. Why should the swinging females continue to plod dismally along with the dull male
ones? Why should the fates of the groovy and the creepy be inter-
twined? Why should the active and imaginative consult the passive and dull on social policy? Why should the independent be
confined to the sewer along with the dependent who need Daddy
to cling to?

A small handful of SCUM can take over the country within a year by systematically fucking up the system, selectively destroying property, and murder:

SCUM will become members of the unwork force, the fuck-up force; they will get jobs of various kinds and unwork. For example, SCUM salesgirls will not charge for merchandise; SCUM telephone operators will not charge for calls; SCUM office and factory workers, in addition to fucking up their work, will secretly destroy equipment. SCUM will unwork at a job until fired, then get a new job to unwork at.

SCUM will forcibly relieve bus drivers, cab drivers and subway token sellers of their jobs and run busses and cabs and dispense free tokens to the public.

SCUM will destroy all useless and harmful objects—cars, store windows, "Great Art," etc.

Eventually SCUM will take over the airwaves—radio and T.V. networks—by forcibly relieving of their jobs all radio and T.V. employees who would impede SCUM's entry into the broadcasting studios.

SCUM will couple bust—barge into mixed (male-female) couples, wherever they are, and bust them up.

SCUM will kill all men who are not in the Men's Auxiliary of SCUM. Men in the Men's Auxiliary are those men who are working diligently to eliminate themselves, men who, regardless of their motives, do good, men who are playing ball with SCUM. A few examples of the men in the Men's Auxiliary are: men who kill men; biological scientists who are working on constructive programs, as opposed to biological warfare; journalists, writers, editors, publishers and producers who disseminate and promote ideas that will lead to the achievement of SCUM's goals; faggots, who by their shimmering, flaming example encourage other men to de-man themselves, and thereby make themselves relatively inoffensive; men who consistently give things away—money, things, services; men who tell it like it is (so far not one ever has), who put women straight, who reveal the truth about themselves, who give the mindless male females correct sentences to parrot, who tell them a woman's primary goal in life would be to squash the male sex (to aid men in this endeavor SCUM will conduct Turd Sessions, at which every male present will give a speech beginning with the sentence: "I am a turd, a lowly, abject turd," then proceed to list all the ways in which he is. His reward for so doing will be the opportunity to fraternize after the session for a whole, solid hour with the SCUM who will be present. Nice, clean-living male women will be invited to the sessions to help clarify any doubts and misunderstandings they may have about the male sex); makers and promoters of sex books and movies, etc., who are hastening the day when all that will be shown on the screen will be Suck and Fuck (males, like the rats following the Pied Piper, will be lured by Pussy to their doom, will be overcome and submerged by and will eventually drown in the passive flesh that they are); drug pushers and advocates, who are hastening the dropping out of men.

Being in the Men's Auxiliary is a necessary but not a sufficient condition for making SCUM's escape list; it's not enough to do good; to save their worthless asses men must also avoid evil. A few examples of the most obnoxious or harmful types are: rapists, politicians and all who are in their service (campaigners, members of political parties, etc.); lousy singers and musicians; Chairmen of Boards; Breadwinners; landlords; owners of greasy spoons and restaurants that play Muzak; "Great Artists"; cheap pikers; cops; tycoons; scientists working on death and destruction programs or for private industry (practically all scientists); liars and phonies; disc jockeys; men who intrude themselves in the slightest way on any strange female; real estate men; stock brokers; men who speak when they have nothing to say; men who loiter idly on the street and mar the landscape with their presence; double-dealers; flimflam artists; litter bugs; plagiarizers; men who in the slightest way harm any female; all men in the advertising industry; dishonest writers, journalists, editors, publishers, etc.;

censors on both the public and private level; all members of the armed forces, including draftees (LBJ and McNamara give orders, but servicemen carry them out) and particularly pilots (If the Bomb drops, LBJ won't drop it; a pilot will). In the case of a man whose behavior falls into both the good and bad categories, an overall subjective evaluation of him will be made to determine if his behavior is, in the balance, good or bad.

It is most tempting to pick off the female "Great Artists," double-dealers, etc. along with the men, but that would be impractical, as there would be no one left; all women have a fink streak in them, to a greater or lesser degree, but it stems from a lifetime of living among men. Eliminate men and women will shape up. Women are improvable; men are not, although their behavior is. When SCUM gets hot on their asses it'll shape up fast.

Simultaneously with the fucking up, looting, couple busting, destroying and killing, SCUM will recruit. SCUM, then, will consist of the recruiters; the elite corps—the hard core activists (the fuckups, looters and destroyers) and the elite of the elite—the killers.

Dropping out is not the answer; fucking up is. Most women are already dropped out; they were never in. Dropping out gives control to those few who don't drop out; dropping out is exactly what the establishment leaders want; it plays into the hands of the enemy; it strengthens the system instead of undermining it, since it is based entirely on the non-participation, passivity, apathy and non-involvement of the mass of women. Dropping out, however, is an excellent policy for men, and SCUM will enthusiastically encourage it.

Looking inside yourself for salvation, contemplating your navel, is not, as the Drop Out people would have you believe, the answer. Happiness lies outside yourself, is achieved through interacting with others. Self-forgetfulness should be one's goal, not self-absorption. The male, capable of only the latter, makes a virtue of an irremediable fault and sets up self-absorption, not only as a good but as a Philosophical Good, and thus gets credit for being deep.

SCUM will not picket, demonstrate, march or strike to attempt to achieve its ends. Such tactics are for nice, genteel ladies who scrupulously take only such action as is guaranteed to be ineffective. In addition, only decent, clean-living, male women, highly trained in submerging themselves in the species, act on a mob basis. SCUM consists of individuals; SCUM is not a mob, a blob. Only as many SCUM will do a job as are needed for the job. Also, SCUM, being cool and selfish, will not subject itself to getting rapped on the head with billy clubs; that's for the nice, "privileged, educated," middle-class ladies with a high regard for and touching faith in the essential goodness of Daddy and policemen. If SCUM ever marches, it will be over LBJ's stupid, sickening face; if SCUM ever strikes, it will be in the dark with a six inch blade.

SCUM will always operate on a criminal as opposed to a civil disobedience basis, that is, as opposed to openly violating the law and going to jail in order to draw attention to an injustice. Such tactics acknowledge the rightness of the overall system and are used only to modify it slightly, change specific laws. SCUM is against the entire system, the very idea of law and government. SCUM is out to destroy the system, not attain certain rights within it. Also, SCUM—always selfish, always cool—will always aim to avoid detection and punishment. SCUM will always be furtive, sneaky, underhanded (although SCUM murders will always be known to be such).

Both destruction and killing will be selective and discriminate. SCUM is against half-crazed, indiscriminate riots, with no clear objective in mind, and in which many of your own kind are picked off. SCUM will never instigate, encourage or participate in riots of any kind or any other form of indiscriminate destruction. SCUM will coolly, furtively, stalk its prey and quietly move in for the kill. Destruction will never be such as to block off routes needed for the transportation of food and other essential supplies, contaminate or cut off the water supply, block streets and traffic to the extent that ambulances can't get through or impede the functioning of hospitals.

SCUM will keep on destroying, looting, fucking up and killing until the money-work system no longer exists and automation is completely instituted or until enough women cooperate with SCUM to make violence unnecessary to achieve these goals, that is, until enough women either unwork or quit work, start looting, leave men and refuse to obey all laws inappropriate to a truly civilized society. Many women will fall into line, but many others, who surrendered long ago to the enemy, who are so adapted to animalism, to maleness, that they like restrictions and restraints, don't know what to do with freedom, will continue to be toadies and doormats, just as peasants in rice paddies remain peasants in rice paddies as one regime topples another. A few of the more volatile will whimper and sulk and throw their toys and dishrags on the floor, but SCUM will continue to steamroller over them.

A completely automated society can be accomplished very simply and quickly once there is a public demand for it. The blueprints for it are already in existence, and its construction will only take a few weeks with millions of people working at it. Even though off the money system, everyone will be most happy to pitch in and get the automated society built; it will mark the beginning of a fantastic new era, and there will be a celebration atmosphere accompanying the construction.

The elimination of money and the complete institution of automation are basic to all other SCUM reforms; without these two the others can't take place; with them the others will take place very rapidly. The government will automatically collapse. With complete automation it will be possible for every woman to vote directly on every issue by means of an electronic voting machine in her house. Since the government is occupied almost entirely with regulating economic affairs and legislating against purely private matters, the elimination of money and with it the elimination of males who wish to legislate "morality" will mean that there will be practically no issues to vote on.

After the elimination of money there will be no further need to kill men; they will be stripped of the only power they have over psychologically independent females. They will be able to impose themselves only on the doormats, who like to be imposed upon. The rest of the women will be busy solving the few remaining unsolved problems before planning their agenda for eternity and Utopia—completely revamping educational programs so that millions of women can be trained within a few months for high level intellectual work that now requires years of training (this can be done very easily once our educational goal is to educate and not to perpetuate an academic and intellectual elite); solving the problems of disease and old age and death and completely redesigning our cities and living quarters. Many women will for a while continue to think they dig men, but as they become accustomed to female society and as they become absorbed in their projects, they will eventually come to see the utter uselessness and banality of the male.

The few remaining men can exist out their puny days dropped out on drugs or strutting around in drag or passively watching the high-powered female in action, fulfilling themselves as spectators, vicarious livers* or breeding in the cow pasture with the toadies, or they can go off to the nearest friendly neighborhood suicide center where they will be quietly, quickly and painlessly gassed to death.

Prior to the institution of automation, to the replacement of males by machines, the male should be of use to the female, wait on her, cater to her slightest whim, obey her every command, be totally subservient to her, exist in perfect obedience to her will, as opposed to the completely warped, degenerate situation we have now of men, not only existing at all, cluttering up the world with their ignominious presence, but being pandered to and groveled before by the mass of females, millions of women piously

---

*It will be electronically possible for him to tune in to any specific female he wants to and follow in detail her every movement. The females will kindly, obligingly consent to this, as it won't hurt them in the slightest and it is a marvelously kind and humane way to treat their unfortunate, handicapped fellow beings.

worshipping the Golden Calf, the dog leading the master on the leash, when in fact the male, short of being a drag queen is least miserable when abjectly prostrate before the female, a complete slave. Rational men want to be squashed, stepped on, crushed and crunched, treated as the curs, the filth that they are, have their repulsiveness confirmed.

The sick, irrational men, those who attempt to defend themselves against their disgustingness, when they see SCUM barreling down on them, will cling in terror to Big Mama with her Big Bouncy Boobies, but Boobies won't protect them against SCUM; Big Mama will be clinging to Big Daddy, who will be in the corner shitting in his forceful, dynamic pants. Men who are rational, however, won't kick or struggle or raise a distressing fuss, but will just sit back, relax, enjoy the show and ride the waves to their demise.